Praise for *Hungry for More*

'Mel can help you find out what you're really hungry for, healing your relationship with food so your whole life can begin... no more turning to food to feed the void!'
BRIGID MOSS, HEALTH DIRECTOR, *RED*

'Mel Wells is giving a voice to the silent struggle billions of women know so well.'
FORBES UNDER 30

'All hail Mel Wells! Mel has amassed an army of loyal goddesses (aka the thousands of readers whose lives have been transformed by her inspirational go-to guide).'
LOOK MAGAZINE

'Mel's new way of thinking will help women end the war on their bodies and embrace their inner Goddess. The self-loving starts here!'
OK! MAGAZINE

'Hungry for More *is a must-read bible for all women seeking more connection and consciousness around their eating and their life. In it, Mel powerfully helps you pinpoint what it is that you are really craving and how you can answer that call now.'*
REBECCA CAMPBELL, SPIRITUAL TEACHER AND BESTSELLING AUTHOR OF *LIGHT IS THE NEW BLACK* AND *RISE SISTER RISE*

'Mel embodies the very thing she teaches – how to heal your relationship with food in order to truly love and accept yourself.'
ATHENA LAZ, COLUMNIST, *COSMOPOLITAN*

'Mel is a master at stripping back what we don't need – the unfulfilling job, dreary relationship and comfort food. We've all been there. Here she reveals how finding your own brand of spirituality is key to a happy life.'

EMMA HIBBS, WELLBEING WRITER, SPIRIT & DESTINY AND HEALTHY MAGAZINES

'A breath of fresh air. My eyes were truly opened after reading this.'

LUCY GORNALL, HEALTH AND FITNESS EDITOR, FIT & WELL MAGAZINE

'Mel Wells is a light in the world. This woman is here to help others reach their highest potential. She reminds us that we can create miracles in our lives.'

DAVID WOLFE, AUTHOR, NUTRITIONIST, PHILANTHROPIST

'I love how Mel gets it. She speaks from the heart and her practical tips and loving humour-filled chat speak straight to mine. Congrats, Mel, on another wonderful book!'

MELISSA HEMSLEY, CHEF AND BESTSELLING AUTHOR OF EAT HAPPY

'Mel is a beautiful, gorgeous, shining light, a healer, a teacher and a dear friend. She's trailblazing a path to help us go deeper into our own connection with our true self. Her insights will help you love yourself and your body more than you ever thought possible, so you can live the life you know you were made for. This book and Mel's teachings can radically transform your life.'

SHANNON KAISER, BESTSELLING AUTHOR OF THE SELF-LOVE EXPERIMENT

'Mel is a true inspiration and a shining light, sharing her authentic self and story to help others create their own wonderful and fulfilling best versions of themselves.'

JULIE MONTAGU, NUTRITIONIST, YOGA TEACHER AND AUTHOR OF FOUR BOOKS INCLUDING EAT REAL FOOD AND RECHARGE

'This book is truly a celebration of conscious cravings. Wise. Witty. Raw. A must read for everyone with an appetite for a soulful and awakened life.'

'Mel is a woman I cherish because of her commitment to her own journey and her willingness to dive into the discomfort in order to share tools with others. Being unfulfilled manifests in so many ways that are detrimental to our health and our relationships – and it is always deceiving because it shows up as addiction, food addiction, procrastination, perfectionism and self-sabotage of just about every kind. In my opinion, this book covers one of the most important topics not only of our time, but for the human spirit.'

'The message of this book resonated with me in a profoundly intimate way – I genuinely couldn't put it down. I learned something new on pretty much every page, and it both inspired and challenged me in equal measure (which is exactly what a great book should do). Mel shares her stories and wisdom with such generosity, clarity and tenderness for the reader, that I often found myself nodding my head along in agreement! The perfect read for anyone ready to embrace the truth of who they really are – and hungry to make the very most of the magnificent gift and opportunity that is their life.'

'Hungry for More is exactly what this industry needs. In the midst of an era where we are so out of tune with our bodies, constantly connected and on the go, yet at the same time desperate to get more from our life, more from our experiences and more than what we look like from the exterior, this book will change lives. Mel is a change maker, an inspiration to modern millennials wanting a fulfilled, conscious life.'

BECKI RABIN, FOUNDER, *ALTERNATIVELY HEALTHY* MAGAZINE

'An absolute must read for women – and men – who are struggling with their food habits, weight and body image and wish to heal those negative relationships. Mel strives to help you realize that you are not alone and, more importantly, not to blame. She's a lifesaver for so many women, and the words in this book are golden.'

ALEX LIGHT, CONTRIBUTOR, *HELLO!* MAGAZINE

Hungry for More

Hungry for More

Satisfy Your Deepest Cravings,
Feed Your Dreams and Live a Full-Up Life

MEL WELLS

HAY HOUSE

Carlsbad, California • New York City
London • Sydney • New Delhi

Published in the United Kingdom by:
Hay House UK Ltd, Astley House, 33 Notting Hill Gate, London W11 3JQ
Tel: +44 (0)20 3675 2450; Fax: +44 (0)20 3675 2451; www.hayhouse.co.uk

Published in the United States of America by:
Hay House Inc., PO Box 5100, Carlsbad, CA 92018-5100
Tel: (1) 760 431 7695 or (800) 654 5126
Fax: (1) 760 431 6948 or (800) 650 5115; www.hayhouse.com

Published in Australia by:
Hay House Australia Ltd, 18/36 Ralph St, Alexandria NSW 2015
Tel: (61) 2 9669 4299; Fax: (61) 2 9669 4144; www.hayhouse.com.au

Published in India by:
Hay House Publishers India, Muskaan Complex, Plot No.3, B-2,
Vasant Kunj, New Delhi 110 070
Tel: (91) 11 4176 1620; Fax: (91) 11 4176 1630; www.hayhouse.co.in

Text © Mel Wells, 2018

The moral rights of the author have been asserted.

The information given in this book should not be treated as a substitute for professional medical advice; always consult a medical practitioner. Any use of information in this book is at the reader's discretion and risk. Neither the author nor the publisher can be held responsible for any loss, claim or damage arising out of the use, or misuse, of the suggestions made, the failure to take medical advice or for any material on third-party websites.

A catalogue record for this book is available from the British Library.

ISBN: 978-1-78817-021-5

Dedicated to Andy, for guiding me home.

Contents

Imagine a Woman

Imagine a woman who believes it is right
and good she is a woman.
A woman who honors her experience and tells her stories.
Who refuses to carry the sins of others
within her body and life.

Imagine a woman who trusts and respects herself.
A woman who listens to her needs and desires.
Who meets them with tenderness and grace.

Imagine a woman who acknowledges the
past's influence on the present.
A woman who has walked through her past.
Who has healed into the present.

Imagine a woman who authors her own life.
A woman who exerts, initiates, and moves on her own behalf.
Who refuses to surrender except to her
truest self and wisest voice.

Imagine a woman who names her own gods.
A woman who imagines the divine in her image and likeness.
Who designs a personal spirituality to inform her daily life.

Imagine a woman in love with her own body.
A woman who believes her body is enough, just as it is.
Who celebrates its rhythms and cycles
as an exquisite resource.

Imagine a woman who honors the body of
the Goddess in her changing body.
A woman who celebrates the accumulation
of her years and her wisdom.
Who refuses to use her life-energy disguising
the changes in her body and life.

Imagine a woman who values the women in her life.
A woman who sits in circles of women.
Who is reminded of the truth about herself when she forgets.

Imagine yourself as this woman.

Patricia Lynn Reilly

How to Get the Most Out of This Book

Side dishes

After most chapters in this book, you will find a series of journaling prompts titled 'Questions to self'. If you're new to journaling, I find that having a few questions to start you off really helps to get things flowing nicely. These questions should help you to uncover more of your soul's truths and deeper cravings. All you need is a journal or notebook, and a pen.

Meditations

I have also created a series of free audio meditations, one to go with each chapter of this book, that you can download at www.melwells.com/hungryformorebonuses.

Personality quiz

If you'd like to understand more about what your relationship with food says about you, how your food patterns relate to your life patterns and how you can improve your relationship with food, take the free quiz at www.melwells.com/quiz.

Chapter 1

Are You Hungry?

'How we digest food is how we digest life.'
DR MARC DAVID

Hunger is one of the most powerful chemical messages sent by the body to the brain. It's a physiological bodily response we all experience that clearly tells us when we need to eat.

And yet so many of us may have lost touch with our body's hunger signals. If you have a history of dieting or disordered eating, you may no longer even be aware of what your body's natural rhythm for hunger even feels like. If you have a history of binge eating, maybe you can't even remember the last time you gave your body a chance to speak to you and let you know when it's genuinely in need of food.

In diet culture we've subtly been taught to ignore our appetites or to 'fight' our cravings, so we tend either to resent our hunger or suppress it, for fear it will lead us astray and down into deep, dark pits of guilt and remorse. We've become confused between our psychological cravings and our bodies' biological need for food.

In not allowing our bodies the chance to speak to us, we tend to be guided by our emotional cravings, which too often lead us to the fridge, the cookie jar, the supermarket, the bottom of an ice cream tub. It isn't our biological hunger that's leading us astray – it's our emotions, our minds. Our emotional cravings aren't brought on by our body; they're caused by psychological needs. This means we may *think* we're craving food, when actually we're craving something much deeper.

So why fight our desire for food when it's our emotions we need to address?

When I was 18, I went completely berserk when my mum casually remarked to herself, 'Whoops! I haven't even had my lunch yet; I completely forgot to eat today!' Blood coursed through my veins and my jaw clenched up. I lost my shit. 'You forgot to eat?' I screamed at her, 'How on Earth can you just forget to eat?' I buried my head in my hands. God, I wished that I could just 'forget to eat'. Food was all I thought about, day in, day out. All I wanted was to be able to eat 'like a normal person', whatever that meant.

More than 10 years later, now a certified eating psychology coach and experienced health coach, I teach women to understand and heal their relationships with food. And the biggest discovery I've made through my work is that it wasn't ever actually about the food.

It was about fulfilment.

Our relationship with food is really a reflection of our relationship with ourselves. So, when we prioritize healing and improving the relationship we have with ourselves, practise deep self-enquiry, and loving and accepting all parts of ourselves, our perceived food cravings often seem to vanish all by themselves, no diet or willpower required. Why? Because to live at peace with food is to live at peace with ourselves, and vice versa: when we find peace within ourselves, we also naturally find peace with food.

This is why healing our relationship with food is not just about finding a balance with our weight – it's about so much more than that. Healing your relationship with food can unlock a doorway to spiritual and emotional growth.

When we are unhappy or unfulfilled, normal eating slides into overeating, undereating or another unhealthy relationship with food. When we don't feel truly fulfilled by our lives, this is when addictive habits creep in. In place of a fulfilled life, we seek out filling up not just through food but through other vices like alcohol, drugs, sex, gambling, shopping, social media and so on.

But when you pursue a fulfilled life, food or other vices stop being your 'happy place'.

You find a deeper pleasure from life than you found at the bottom of the ice cream tub. (I'm speaking from experience.)

Leading a fulfilled life requires a little more effort and self-enquiry, of course. It requires willingness to change, grow and push yourself outside your comfort zone. It requires a willingness to get radically real with yourself and dive deep into your awareness. It requires oodles of self-love.

Of course, it's much easier to download a meal plan or another quick fix than it is to pursue a fulfilled life. It's much easier to keep starting and failing diets every Monday, searching for that 'magic pill', than it is to be honest about your true cravings and dive deep into your soul.

When people want to lose weight, they often go on a crash diet – or they do something else. I am all about that something else.

And that something else is: changing your life. Making a shift. Overhauling your belief system. Loving yourself. Getting happy. Changing your environment. The ones who are doing this aren't going on another diet that makes them starving and miserable – they're doing real soul work on themselves, and the food and weight problems naturally shift themselves as a byproduct. These people glow with happiness, inner confidence and fulfillment.

That's the something else I'm talking about.

And you're here, aren't you? So I'm assuming you're ready for that something else, too.

So – shall we?

> **What you think is a body problem**
> **is actually a mind problem.**
>
> **What you think is a food problem**
> **is actually a life problem.**

How many times have you found yourself mindlessly looking in the fridge for answers, or ravaging a packet of crisps when you're stressed, or ploughing through food when, actually, you weren't even hungry in the first place? All you had to tune in, and get aware.

You were hungry all right, but not for food.

That's right, you were hungry for more.

As you've got this far, I'm going to presume that one or more of the following points apply to you:

❀ You sometimes feel like something is missing in your life – you just can't put your finger on what.

❀ You like to believe in synchronicity and that everything happens for a reason.

❀ A fulfilled life sounds much more appealing to you than another new diet or regime does.

❀ You're somewhat curious about your spirituality but, if you're honest, you're also kind of cynical, a little bit intimidated or overwhelmed by it all.

❀ You've faced some challenges surrounding your relationship with food or cravings and you're keen to uncover the hidden messages revealing what this could be leading you to explore within yourself.

❀ Sometimes your cravings are so strong you feel like something possesses you.

❀ You often feel like you are suppressing parts of yourself or like you're not living to your fullest potential.

❀ You sometimes feel like the people around you don't really understand or get you.

❀ You want to learn how you can work in harmony with the Universe, to help you...

　　~ Become completely at peace with yourself

　　~ Understand and satisfy your deeper cravings in life

　　~ Create a fulfilled life that you love and that makes you want to jump out of bed in the morning

(I mean, who wouldn't want to know all of that? Nobody, that's who.)

If you're someone, like me, who has struggled with their relationship with food, I want to gently remind you:

It's not about the food.

It's never been about the food.

That's right, sweet goddess, I am here to suggest that your soul's desires go far deeper than a bag of salty pretzels or a big glass of Shiraz at the end of the day. If your relationship with food and cravings has been an ongoing theme in your life, trust me when I say:

**Every challenge you face in life
is an invitation to go deeper into
the truth of who you are.**

Throughout this book I will share my stories, but also try to help you figure out exactly what it is you're hungry for, and what you can do to fill that void from the inside out, rather than continually trying to feed it from the outside in – which never amounts to any true sustenance or nourishment.

We are all truly hungry for:

* Connection

* Intimacy

* Freedom

* Purpose

❖ Belonging

❖ Deeper meaning in life

❖ Creativity

❖ Adventure

❖ Lasting pleasure

❖ Self-expression

❖ Love

Some readers will say to themselves, 'This all sounds great Mel, but to be honest I just want to know what to eat and what not to eat. Can't you tell me how to lose weight instead?' Yes, yes – I know. I thought more food rules were the answers for a long time, too. For years I chased that illusion. Only when I began to realize that my answers didn't lie in *what* I ate, but in *why* I ate, *how* I ate, and my *relationship* with food, did I transform. Only when I began to stop asking the question *How can I lose weight?* and instead started asking, *How can I enrich my life?* did things shift.

**Only when I began to focus on filling
up my life did I stop constantly needing
to fill up my plate and my stomach.**

In my first book, *The Goddess Revolution*, we explored our relationship with food and why diet culture is so damaging not only to our physical health, but to our mental and emotional wellbeing too. We had the kind of conversations around food, diets and body image that help us understand ourselves more – and slowly but surely, we began to peel back the layers of our complex relationships with food and with our bodies, and to embrace a lifestyle of self-love.

So what's next?

When we're brave enough to begin to explore our relationship with food, we're also forced to ask deeper, more meaningful questions about ourselves and our lives. And things begin to reveal themselves – about our happiness, our close relationships, our career choices, our higher purpose, our connection with the divine.

When you commit to going deeper into these messages and truly open yourself up to exploring them with curiosity, you can discover the hidden architectures of the Universe and unlock a gateway to personal, emotional and spiritual growth and freedom. Many of us go through our lives ignoring or denying the wisdom of the Universe that so often speaks through the body and through our relationship with food. But now we're paying attention.

Hungry for More is here to help you become your own detective and get to work on the best and most rewarding odyssey you'll ever embark on – self-discovery.

When you're working on your relationship with food, you're really working on your relationship with yourself. And when you're working on your relationship with yourself, you're really working on the relationship you have with life. When you work on the relationship you have with life, you're really working on your relationship with the Universe. And when you get to the heart of what you've been craving all along, you can begin to truly satisfy your deeper cravings and move forward with confidence, joy and unconditional self-love. Your personal growth will accelerate. You will fall madly in love with yourself and your life. And you will feel connected to a higher version of yourself, and to a higher power that helps you to make all your dreams and visions come to life, before your very eyes.

This is a calling for the ones who are hungry for more.

Chapter 2

You, Food
and the
Universe

'All of us are seeking the same thing. We share the desire to fulfill the highest, truest expression of ourselves as human beings.'

OPRAH WINFREY

So, what in the Goddess' name does your relationship with food have to do with the Universe?

Yes, I keep mentioning the Universe, don't I? Now, if this is the kind of thing that freaks you out, don't worry. I'm not about to start asking you to carry crystals in your bra or practise transcendental meditation for two hours a day. (Although, you can absolutely do both of these things if you want to.) I've personally gone through phases in my life ranging from feeling completely disconnected from any higher power to feeling completely in tune and like I'm being guided with practically every step I take. When I say 'the Universe', I'm talking about the magic that's in all of us, that exists beyond our five senses. That voice that speaks to you, or offers you signs. Those coincidences that you know, deep down, are not actually coincidences at all. The Universe is not separate from you; it's what you and I are both made of, so when we work with the Universe, what this really means, on a fundamental level, is that we're working with the innermost, wisest part of our souls.

We're working with our higher self, which is, in other words, our truest self.

Our spiritual health is integral to how we operate in the world. When we feel connected to something higher than ourselves, whatever our religious or spiritual belief may be, we move through our lives with faith, with trust and with purpose. We find more meaning in life, and we feel more connected.

You can make your spiritual practice whatever you want it to be. Even self-awareness is a spiritual practice. Getting to know yourself is a spiritual practice. Trust is a spiritual practice. Your yoga, your favourite workout or just your morning routine could be your spiritual practice. Your spirituality is simply your being aware of your true, or higher, self, which is loving, compassionate and free.

When we look at healing our relationship with food, our challenges often lie around control, and control may also be what's held you back from spirituality in the past. If you really love being in control, like I used to, then the idea of spirituality can sound nice enough, but ain't nobody making you surrender or actually let go of your control. Your spirituality is about *actually letting go* of that control – even just a little bit – not just saying it. It's about learning to trust yourself, your path, your life.

While controlling things can feel good in the moment, because it makes us feel safe, ultimately it leads us to us feeling *out of control* and *unsafe* when one tiny thing doesn't go to plan. When we try to perfectly plan our lives, perfectly control our food or perfectly control our love life, we are living from a place of fear. We're not opening ourselves up to a higher power – in fact, we're blocking it.

Dieting, of course, is all rooted in fear and control.

We don't check in with our bodies intuitively, instead we turn to control. But you can change your fear-based story to a love-based story. When you can learn how to trust your body, you can learn how to trust yourself, and trust the Universe too.

How often do you eat when your body isn't actually hungry at all? More often than not, our emotions come into play in a big way. Depending on what's going on in our lives, we can become fixated on food, develop emotional-eating or binge-eating tendencies; or, on the other end of the spectrum, we can purposely avoid or restrict food as a way to deal with a conflict we're having within ourselves.

If you've ever wondered how 'normal people' eat – well, they listen to their bodies. They eat when they're hungry and they stop when they're full. That's intuitive eating. And intuitive eating is how we were all designed to eat. Just like every other animal on this planet was. We work best when we listen to our bodies, are in tune with ourselves, our body's signals, and with nature, and we're not trying to control and manipulate the whole darn thing.

The biggest way we interfere with hunger is with our minds. Our minds are what we need to master. This is where all of our obstacles lie when it comes to food. The body is a physical reflection of where our mind is at, and the choices we make in our minds over a period of time. So the solution is not in dieting or even more nutrition knowledge, but in transforming our mindset and awareness. The key to restoring balance is to transform unconscious habits that are into choices made by being self-aware.

What actually makes us healthy?

Health isn't all about salads and treadmills (much as I would have liked to think it was, in the past). Your health and 'being healthy' is about a much bigger picture than that. Health is broken down into six major components – in no particular order:

❖ Physical health

❖ Mental health

❖ Emotional health

❖ Environmental health

❖ Social health

❖ Spiritual health

In other words, it's not just about what you're putting into your body and how often you're moving it (physical health). It's also about how healthy your mind is and how positive or, by contrast, self-destructive your thoughts are and how well you're able to process and cope with the demands of daily life (mental health). It's about how healthy your relationships are and how you conduct and express yourself in them (social health), and it's about how you handle your feelings (emotional health). It's about the environment you live in, and how safe you feel living in it (environmental health). And lastly, it's about your sense of purpose and fulfilment in life, and your relationship with a power greater than yourself (spiritual health).

We can't always be in perfect health; often we're playing a balancing act. But it's important to look at all six components and get radically honest with ourselves. So many of us become fixated on weight loss and 'How to drop pounds' but only pursue changing our physical health. We often turn a blind eye to everything that's not about literally changing our physical body. We fail to look at our mental health, emotional health, environmental health, social health and spiritual health. Many of us find it unnerving to look at our eating habits, only to discover there's a lot more at play. *Darn it, can't we keep eating separate from relationships, money or family issues?* 'Fraid not, sister.

I'm here to tell you that your answers actually lie in all of these components, and the question is not 'How do I lose weight?' but 'How can I become healthier, happier and more fulfilled?' When your internal world is healed, your body can find its natural place. When your life is a fulfilled one, you won't be using food to fill in all the gaps. And so your body does change physically; it's just a more thorough, lasting process. And physical change isn't the end goal; it's just a natural byproduct.

Healthy self – heal thyself

In order to become truly healthy, we must identify what heals us. What heals us is:

❖ Love

❖ Connection

❖ Relationships

❖ Warmth

❖ Play/fun

❖ Light

- Art/music

- Creativity

- Purpose and meaning

- Nature

- Family

- Home

- Togetherness

- Belonging

What we are after here is full nourishment: we must not only nourish the body with good food, but also nourish the mind with knowledge, the heart with love and the spirit with awareness, faith and trust. I invite you to ask yourself continually about what *really* nourishes you?

Questions to self

- *In my life, what nourishes my mind?*

- *What nourishes my body?*

- *What nourishes my soul?*

- *What elements of my health may I have been overlooking or neglecting, and why?*

- *My relationship with food is ...*

Your relationship with food is a mirror to your life.

Chapter 3

Hungry to Be Free, Hungry to Be Me

*'You are the world. When you transform yourself,
the world you live in will also be transformed.'*

DEEPAK CHOPRA

Ever since I was a young girl, I have highly valued my freedom and unwillingness to join the crowd. I can remember being at school and deciding to make up my own rules for how I would get by. I knew that as long as I got the homework in on time and continually got good grades, I could get away with skipping class whenever I needed to.

Why? To follow my dreams. I knew from a very early age that I had zero desire to get a normal job or live 'a normal life'. For me, that was just never an option. I was an extremely expressive kid, with huge ambition and self-belief. My dream was always to act, to be on stage, to perform for people. Doing that was my first experience of a 'flow state' – being in such bliss, so present, that I lost any sense of ego or who I was. I would lose myself in the moment.

What I will always appreciate about my mum is that she always supported that, and never made me miss an audition for the sake of schoolwork – my dreams always came first. So if that meant pretending I had flu, or a family emergency, or a dentist's appointment, so I could zip off to an audition, so be it. I would do my homework in the back of the car while simultaneously changing into a leotard and tights, eating pasta out of a Tupperware box on my lap, all within the space of 30 minutes – the time it took to get from the school gates to my dance or drama classes each night. I guess she taught me that if I worked hard, I could be anything I wanted to. I skipped a lot of school, but always handed in my work on time so I wouldn't get in trouble for it, even if it meant getting up at 5 a.m. to finish it the morning of the deadline.

My mum and dad were both entrepreneurs, designing their lives around their passions. My dad was a psychologist and hypnotherapist who saw clients in his home office, and my mum created a series of small businesses that she ran from home – learning packs for children, school holiday activity camps, then aromatherapy and beauty therapy. I learned through osmosis that I was free to create whatever life I wanted for myself. And I could work for myself if I wanted to. No dream was too big or unrealistic.

I left school as soon as they would let me out of the gates for good, and went straight into the performing arts world – but this was where my food problems began. I wasn't equipped for the competitive, bitchy nature the performance industry can so often bring out in teenage girls, and I lost so much confidence trying to fit in and be liked. Stopping eating was a metaphor for stopping loving myself, stopping valuing myself, stopped allowing myself pleasure or happiness. Eating disorders are highly addictive, and in a twisted way they make you feel successful and accomplished. You know it's a problem, but you still feel like you're winning or in control, even when you're far from it.

Even when I landed a great TV job I couldn't fully immerse myself in it, because I was obsessed with food instead, and so insecure about how I appeared onscreen. This job saw me change location and environment, which triggered my disorder to transcend from not eating at all to eating everything in sight. This led to extreme guilt, shame and self-loathing. Before I knew it, I was an extreme bulimic, abusing my body with junk food, diet pills, vomiting and laxatives. I pushed my family away. Food had taken over my relationships, my dreams, my life.

No matter how much I tried to fill myself up with food, I couldn't shake off the feeling of emptiness.

I had landed the job of my dreams, so why did I feel so trapped, so unfulfilled, so alone? I was desperate to feel free in my body, but all I did was turn to more control, more rules, more willpower – which was always so short-lived. I felt like I was fighting a losing battle with myself.

As my mum drove us through the Cotswolds on the way to see my first eating disorder therapist, the atmosphere was tense. I could sense my mum was pinning her hopes on this appointment to fix me, even though she was calmly saying to me, 'Now, just be completely honest with her. And if you don't like it after one session, we can just go home.'

I sat down on the therapist's couch like a meek little mouse and completely baffled as to what this strange woman was going to ask of me. She was an older woman, with wise, loving eyes that made me feel a little bit uncomfortable, like she could see straight into my soul and if I dared to try to fib to her, she would see through me and call me out at once.

She asked me one question and the floodgates opened. I poured my heart out to her and, between sobs, told her what a mess I was in with my food and my body. She allowed me to cry until I had run out of steam. Then she calmly took my hand, led me out to the hallway and asked me to look at a framed poem on the wall. She asked me to read it out. Through sobs and sniffles, I read:

Our deepest fear is not that we are inadequate.

*Our deepest fear is that we are
powerful beyond measure.*

It is our light, not our darkness, that most frightens us.

*We ask ourselves, Who am I to be brilliant,
gorgeous, talented, fabulous?*

Actually, who are you not to be?

You are a child of God.

Your playing small doesn't serve the world.

*There is nothing enlightened about shrinking so
that other people won't feel insecure around you.*

We are all meant to shine, as children do.

*We were born to make manifest the
glory of God that is within us.*

*It is not just in some of us; it is in everyone
and as we let our own light shine,*

*We unconsciously give others
permission to do the same.*

*As we are liberated from our own fear, our
presence automatically liberates others.*

MARIANNE WILLIAMSON

This is a very famous text and its author, spiritual teacher Marianne Williamson, is now one of my heroines. I see the beauty in this message, and in many ways I try to live by these words and teachings. But back then? I did not follow whatsoever. *What the hell,* I thought. *This therapist woman I'm seeing is a freak. How on earth is a poem about God going to help me get my food under control?* Devastated, I blankly stared at this poem on the wall, then back at the therapist. I wiped the tears and snot away from my face as I realized that I had poured my heart out to someone who just didn't understand me at all. This woman was surely round the bend. I didn't need a poem – I needed help. How, pray tell, would this poem make me control my food, lose weight, conquer an eating disorder and make me happy again? I couldn't for the life of me connect the dots. I walked away from that therapy session completely deflated and downtrodden, feeling more lost and misunderstood than ever.

All I wanted was for someone to fix me and for it to be easy.

More than anything I wanted to be free from this vicious cycle that dominated my life.

But I wasn't ready to listen; I wasn't ready to open my mind or to rely on anything but my own strength, my ego – and my own illusions of control. For years after that day, I carried on struggling by myself, trying to fill myself up with food, dieting and weight loss and relying solely on my own willpower to try to 'fix' myself. I carried on losing and gaining the same weight over and over for years, trying to maintain control. Only later was I able to see the importance of this poem, this lesson, this magic. But at the time, I wasn't ready for the lesson. I was addicted to my own stories, my victimhood, my suffering.

It was during this time that I met my ex-husband. He was everything my childhood Disney-princess fantasies had been made of: strong, handsome, heroic, a military man. In many ways I felt like he had rescued me from myself, and the love I felt from him definitely calmed down my demons to some extent. It was somewhat proof that I was worthy of love. But I hadn't learned to love myself first. I hadn't learned yet that I needed to become my own hero.

Within a few months we were engaged, but I was just 20 years old and still very much in the throes of bulimia, albeit slightly more controlled than previous years. It was an addiction I had kept under wraps from him, and although he noticed a few small things, he would never bring it up with me – I just don't think he knew what to say or how to handle it. Emotional intimacy and close communication were not strengths in our relationship, although they may have seemed so on the outside, and I was happy to keep hiding, pretending everything was fine.

Two years and two Afghanistan tours later, we had a big white wedding and moved to an idyllic country farmhouse that belonged to his family. I was now working as a model, driving up and down the country for jobs and sometimes going abroad. I guess my job looked quite shiny and glamorous on the outside, but on the inside it felt soulless. I still felt completely trapped in my body, needing to fit measurements required for clients, losing weight for jobs, squeezing myself into dresses that didn't fit my natural shape and constantly dieting for shoots, absolutely terrified of gaining weight. My measurements weren't allowed to fluctuate in that way that all bodies naturally do.

Have you ever looked at someone else's life and thought, She looks like she must be so happy?

Well, to be honest, I used to look at my own life like that, and wonder who on Earth that woman was – and where the real me was hiding. I had a man that loved me, a beautiful, stable home, and I was making a decent living from a fairly cool job. But I felt trapped. Alone. Misunderstood. Isolated. I was living in an area that made me feel like I was standing still. The few friends I had real connections with were nowhere near me, and I struggled to find any real common ground with the other wives and girlfriends I met. At dinners and events, I felt like I had to behave in a certain way that wasn't true to me. Nobody wanted to talk about the kinds of topic I wanted to talk about, so I found myself trying to fit in, trying to make myself small so I wouldn't stand out too much or upset anyone.

We argued every day. I felt like the more I tried to be my true self, the more the marriage failed, and the more I fitted inside the box and played the role I thought I 'should' play, behaved myself and got on with it, the better the marriage became. I felt like I had been slotted into the wrong life, a life meant for another woman – not me. And the hardest thing to accept was that I had happily chosen all of it. Had I not been present for every single moment up to this point? All of these things I had chosen? All of these things I had planned? So why was I dreaming of running away and starting a new life altogether?

I felt like something was missing, and I didn't know why. Everything on the surface looked so perfect. But I couldn't understand why I felt like I was playing a part, rather than just being myself. I remember thinking to myself, *I know this isn't the real me, but there'll be time for the real me later. Later I'll create a world for myself. But this is safe, this is comfortable and I really don't want to upset anyone. It isn't that bad. Really, I should just be grateful.*

Have you ever been in a relationship that you knew deep down was wrong, but thought that if you threw things at it, in blind denial, that something would magically fix it and make you happy again? This was what I began to do. We started renovating and decorating the house, creating a perfect home. I had my own office, bathroom and kitchen that I got to design myself, two gorgeous Bengal cats that felt like part of the furniture.

One day in the bathroom, both of us covered in paint, he held two off-white swatches up to a wall. 'Which one for this wall, Mel?' I looked at the swatches. My heart sank. Inside, I said to myself, *Neither. I don't give a damn which swatch for the wall. Because I don't want to live in this house. I don't want this life!*

'The left swatch,' I said out loud. Then burst into tears and ran out of the room.

What I find fascinating to reflect on, years later, is that only through healing my relationship with food did I finally find the confidence to stand up for myself and be honest with how I was truly feeling in my relationship. Because healing my relationship with food meant healing my relationship with myself. I hadn't yet learned how to be my own love or have a healthy relationship with myself – I hadn't found peace within myself, so I struggled to be at peace at all.

When having children became a topic of conversation for us – and it was something I seriously considered to fix our relationship (nope, wrong again!) – I had a eureka moment that changed my life. I realized that if I cared about being a mother one day, which I did, then I would have to be a role model. How could I make it through a pregnancy, harming my body in the way that I was doing? How could I truly love another, when I couldn't even love myself?

I have now learned, from the women I've helped for the past five years, that you cannot change your patterns unless you genuinely want to and are ready to give up your illusions of control. And up until we started discussing children, I can honestly say that I wasn't ready to surrender. I wasn't ready to change. And most people for the most part don't actually want to change; they just want to justify staying the same. For a long time I pretended I wanted to heal, when really all I wanted to do was find a different way to lose weight and be in control.

I went on a self-love mission. Surrendering control was the first step. This saw me chucking out the scales, abandoning all diets and making friends with carbohydrates again. I did exercise only when I wanted to, not because of guilt or self-punishment. I remembered how to trust my body and eat when I was actually hungry.

I began to hear the whispers of my body speaking to me, and for the first time in years, I was listening.

Next came facing my fears. I knew that I had to be willing to face my long-standing fear of gaining weight. I had to look it square in the eye and say, *I see you, but I'm choosing freedom. I see you, but I'm choosing happiness. I see you, but I'm willing to step out of my comfort zone, and walk in the direction of what scares me, in order to heal and to grow.*

I started to become uber self-aware, constantly checking in with myself, observing my feelings, patterns and behaviours. *What does this trigger in me? What would my old self have done? What does my new, higher self choose instead?*

At the time, I wasn't aware I was taking these steps – it's only now that I can look back and realize that this is what it really took to overcome my demons. An absolute, strong *why*, a compelling reason to change, a willingness to surrender, to face my fears and be willing to trust my body again – and a lot of self-awareness and self-compassion.

This takes time and patience, but through constant practice and oodles of self-love and forgiveness, you can radically shift your identity to become a new you, a you who chooses positively and wisely for yourself. You can reprogramme your patterns, one by one, by observing your thoughts and feelings then consciously choosing how you want to feel instead.

If freedom is what you desire, then ask yourself, What will make me feel most free?

If loving yourself is what you desire, then ask yourself, *What would someone who loves themselves do?* If you desire to be more confident, then ask yourself, *What would someone who is confident do?* Yes, this is scary and requires you to purposely step outside of your comfort zone, but this is where you will shift your identity and grow into the person you want to become. This is now what I teach in my programme, as this is the practice that has dramatically changed my life.

Choosing freedom

It is extremely important to remember to love yourself intensely throughout this process, and be your own cheerleader. When I committed to doing this with food, everything shifted. It was the first time I'd followed my freedom instead of choosing control. When I chose freedom, incredible shifts began to happen in my life. So? I learned to keep doing it.

Every time I felt fear or judgement around food, a comment or a situation, I would lovingly observe my thoughts, be curious about them, blast them with love, then decide to choose freedom and love instead. Every time I noticed an old pattern, I would consciously decide to choose to do the opposite of what my old self would have done.

I began to rewrite every single pattern I used to have around food. I began to choose to write a different story for my life.

It was terrifying at first, but I realized that if you want to transform, you have to do something different. And often that something different involves you getting not just uncomfortable, but scared. I learned that if I wanted to transcend my fears, I had to step into them and face them, not run away from them.

When I realized I was able to transcend years of bulimia (that I thought I'd always just be stuck with) by changing the way

I thought about myself and consistently choosing to take a higher perspective, suddenly it became clear to me that by mastering my thoughts, my life could become whatever I wanted it to be.

I became a master at daring myself to be braver every day. I became a master at giving myself pep talks, cheering myself on and being my own best friend.

Doing this work on my relationship with myself came to heal me more than I ever imagined possible. Not only did my relationship with food become more magical, but my relationship with everything and everyone in my life became more magical. I realized that I was the creator of my own life. Nobody else: me. So really, the only question left was: what did I want to create?

Around the time I began to realize this and find my own power again, my then sister-in-law said something that really made an impact on me. She said, 'I feel sorry for you Mel because you're just not satisfied with a normal life; you're always hungry for more. I hope one day you find what you're looking for.' Ouch. But she was right. I didn't want a 'normal' life. I wasn't happy.

After thinking long and hard about this exchange, I eventually came to realize what it was I wanted more of, what it was that I was looking for and why I wasn't satisfied in that chapter of my 'normal' life.

It was a craving to be more free. And it was a craving to be more me.

Freedom was what I truly craved.
Freedom to just live – and be myself.

I had no idea how that even looked anymore, but I knew it was out there waiting for me if I was brave enough to go after it. I couldn't explain why or how I knew this; I just knew, deep in my gut, that I was not living in the truest expression of myself. I knew I was suppressing parts of me: the wild woman, the adventurer, the free spirit; the woman who didn't apologize or tread on eggshells around people so as not to upset them or cause any arguments.

Although my life may have looked great on the outside, it didn't feel good on the inside. And that was far more important. And wow, did that realization hit me like a ton of bricks.

The way I understand it now is that a major reason most of us aren't satisfied with our lives is not that we're not grateful for what we already have. It's that we don't feel free enough to be ourselves. We feel some degree of being trapped or unable to express ourselves – whether that's in our bodies, our environments, our relationships or our careers.

Look at where you feel trapped. It's likely not because you're ungrateful, but because your life isn't fully allowing you to be yourself.

When I would diet and lose a few pounds, it was never enough. I was never satisfied. I had to lose another five pounds, then another five pounds – then another five pounds *just to be sure* I wasn't going to gain it all back (which of course, inevitably, I always did). I felt trapped in my own body, and in my mind weight-loss would give me what I so desired: freedom. It would make me more free to be comfortable in my own skin, and therefore free to be fully myself and to step into true happiness and a fulfilled life. But the more pounds I dropped, the more I would ask myself, *So when is this freedom and happiness thing going to come? I don't get it: I lost the weight – why do I still hate my body? Why do I still feel trapped? Why do I still want to cover up with baggy clothes?* I had attached the reward to the outcome. I had attached freedom to a number on the scales – and it hadn't come through.

But feeling unhappy with my body was just a metaphor for feeling unhappy with my life: I felt trapped in my body and I felt trapped in my life. And just as I wanted to cover up my body with baggy clothes, I felt like I was hiding myself away, hiding the real me. Only did I find *true* freedom in my body by allowing myself to simply *be free* in the here and now, in the body I had naturally been given, at the size it naturally wanted to be, with no weight loss required. Crazy concept, right?

Freedom is not something you have to fight for, or achieve, or earn after you've suffered for it. Freedom is not something that comes with a number on a scale or a salary rise. Freedom is something you can claim for yourself, right now. I found freedom in my own body when I stopped dieting and trying to lose weight altogether and just decided I was already free, and that the only person trapping me was… me.

Your life, your choices

Do you believe you're allowed to have freedom in all areas of your life?

Do you believe you're allowed to have what you really want?

Do you believe you don't ever have to settle for a life that doesn't feel like yours?

Do you believe you can have all the freedom in the world – and on your terms?

It's true: essentially, we all want to feel more free in some way or other. We hate feeling caged or trapped. This can show up in a number of ways. It might be the case that we don't feel able to express who we really are in certain groups of people, or that we hide particular parts of ourselves, for fear of being judged or criticized, which can lead to us wanting more freedom to be ourselves. It might be that we've somehow made ourselves feel trapped by a relationship or a job where, again, we feel like we're not the ones actively calling the shots for our own lives. We feel like we're just going along with something. In a relationship, not feeling free may feel like we're going along with everything the other person wants to do, making them and their desires the most important thing while neglecting ourselves and what we truly want. Or perhaps we unconsciously go along with what we think society wants of us or what we think our families and friends want – not stopping to think about what it is that we truly want. What our souls truly want.

When we give up something, such as parts of ourselves for someone else, we call it a compromise, but often what ends up happening is that we feel trapped and resent that other person for 'making us' give it up – and we start craving the freedom to be ourselves again. Similarly, it might be that you're in a job that gives you no freedom to pursue your passions or spend time with loved ones. And so the job gets blamed. But who chose the job?

Whichever area of your life you'd like more freedom in, realize that you're already free.

Yes. You are free. Seriously – you're free to choose again.

What does freedom around food and in your body look like? No rules, no restrictions, no being trapped by diets – instead, the freedom to take responsibility for your own choices. Freedom to take back your power around your food. And it's the same in life. To live an abundant, free life, we must first recognize that we are already free.

Let me ask you something. Do you feel like you're the leading lady in your own life? No, really – do you? If your life were a movie, would you be in the starring role? How does that even look? Is that a scary concept for you to imagine? Maybe your life is actually revolving around someone else's dreams and you're the supportive friend, or actor, or just an extra in the background of the movie, when really you should be the star of the show.

It's your life. *It's your life.*

When you don't speak up for the things that matter to you, that's when your freedom ends. You have to recognize that you are responsible for every single choice you make – throughout your day, throughout your week, throughout your year and throughout your life. Recognize that you are in charge of your stories, your thoughts, your energy, your choices, which means you – nobody else: you – are the one actively creating your own life.

> **When I realized this, I started designing my life on purpose, instead of just reacting to it.**

With every choice you make, ask yourself:

Is this making me feel more free?

Is this making me feel more *me*?

Is this expansive?

Does this feel good in my heart – or is my soul crying out for me not to do this?

**The ones who feel the most free
are the ones who consistently listen
to their heart and follow it.**

They are the ones listening to that intuitive pull and allowing it to guide them.

Yes, freedom takes courage. But only you can give yourself that gift.

Believe in miracles

*'There are only two ways to live your life. One
is as though nothing is a miracle. The other
is as though everything is a miracle.'*
ALBERT EINSTEIN

Since you've got this far, I trust you're someone who is open to explore the possibilities of their mind. I trust you're someone who is fascinated by life's little signs, tests, nudges and lessons. I trust you're someone whose intuition is one of her favourite superpowers.

I therefore invite you not to fight the spiritual side of yourself, or to deny it, but to embrace wholeheartedly the fact that you are a spiritual being having a human experience, not a human who has a 'sometimes spiritual' side to them.

If it doesn't resonate with you when I refer to 'the Universe', feel free to replace this with 'Higher Power', 'Spirit', 'Source', 'God', 'Goddess' or whatever your preference. A lot of us still aren't fully on board with the G-word. But it's all fundamentally the same thing: having belief in something greater than us, and finding purpose and meaning in our existence. It's also about surrendering control and leaning into trust, knowing that what's meant for us won't miss us. It's a deep knowledge that we are safe, and recognizing that incredible things can happen for us in this lifetime when we don't try to control them.

You may have been brought up in an environment that didn't support spirituality. Maybe you're confused about faith. Maybe you grew up going to church then decided as an adult that none of that made sense anymore and now you're not really sure what does make sense. Maybe you recently started following signs, listening to that inner voice. Whatever your stance, realize it's all perfect, it's all valid and it's all part of the same conversation.

> **There are two ways we can live our lives. The first is how most of us begin: we believe that everything is happening <u>to</u> us, that we are victims of our own circumstance and 'life isn't fair'. The second is when we wake up and realize that everything is happening <u>for</u> us – for our greater good, for us to learn, to grow, and to expand to become the greatest versions of ourselves.**

This is when we see miracles in everything. And we don't just *believe* in miracles – we live our lives *knowing* that miracles are present around us at every interaction. We marvel in life's beauty at every opportunity. We do not 'fail'; we learn and grow. And this is down to…? A trust in the bigger picture. Feeling safe in the hands of the Universe. Knowing that we are protected – and loved. This isn't about pretending that there's no pain in the world or that nothing bad ever happens, but rather choosing not to suffer as a result of it, and to turn our wounds into power and wisdom from which we can learn.

If this sounds corny to you, take it in small doses when it suits you. This doesn't have to be a big life overhaul, this can just be a new perspective to take in those little moments of need. And those little moments add up. Next time you find yourself complaining, ask yourself if you can find gratitude instead. Next time you slip into 'Why me?' mode, see if you can instead find the beauty in the lesson that's being presented to you. When you expect miracles, they'll show up. And when you don't expect them, they won't.

So maybe your inspirational quotes on Instagram aren't well received by your nearest and dearest; perhaps they're sniggered at. Maybe you've got yourself some oracle cards or mentioned 'the Universe' in passing, and got an eye-roll from your boyfriend. I get it. I really, really do. But you don't have to wear all white and start converting the masses. This isn't an invitation to go up into the mountains, become a nun and meditate for 20 years to reach enlightenment.

This is an invitation for you to go deeper into the truth of who you are, and ask yourself powerful questions to begin to unlock your true potential.

And as you're reading this book – well, the truth is you've already begun this process.

Be prepared to let your old self die

When I quit my old patterns around food, I was a mess at first. No, seriously. I was a wreck. It wasn't all self-love and expansion the very next day. It was actually as terrifying as hell.

The truth was, I didn't know who I was without a diet or a set of food rules to follow on a Monday morning. It's sad but true. My life for the past seven years had revolved around my starting weight, current weight and goal weight. I turned to diets and food control to feel whole and complete. And when I crumbled, it was binges and overeating that comforted me, followed by a big serving of self-loathing and vowing to start a new diet – on Monday, of course.

Dieting and weight loss had become part of my identity. If I didn't have some big event to try to lose weight for, I felt like I was standing still. I had lost myself in counting, tracking, numbers, systems, pounds, calories and points.

When one quits an addictive pattern after doing it for so long, one can easily slip into chaos. Everything that was so perfectly controlled is now completely gone – you have abundant freedom and your choices are limitless. And that's terrifying. So we panic. And we stress out. And we feel out of control.

I had become addicted to my eating disorder: *Who the hell am I without this addiction?* So many times I wanted to run back to it – it felt safe. Instead, I ran the other way – towards my freedom. But I was shit-scared the whole time.

Suddenly, I had all this freedom and I didn't know what to do with it. I was eating whatever I wanted, with no rules. I chucked out all the clothes I'd been holding onto for when I reached my 'goal weight', and started wearing clothes that fitted my body and made me feel great right now.

But now that my life wasn't consumed by numbers and tracking, now it wasn't consumed with self-hatred and crying in the mirror, now it wasn't consumed with hours of exercise each day – what next?

> **I had a period of time – probably a few months – where I was fighting the urge to go back to the scales, and back to my bulimia, on a daily basis.**

My old behaviours felt so safe. They felt like who I was, so without them I felt lost and out of control. Sitting in the void without my coping mechanism was painful. I was fighting the urge to start restricting again; fighting the urge after every big meal to be sick, or to over-exercise the next day. But deep down in my soul, I knew that the seven years I had spent doing all of these things were *not* working for me, were *not* making me happy, and were definitely *not* helping me to love myself. So why would I go back there? Why would it suddenly be different now?

I knew in my soul I needed to sit in this discomfort, this void of darkness, this unknown, trusting that I was following my freedom and that I was healing. Even if I was gaining weight, I was also gaining back my life. My eating disorder had become so wrapped up in my identity that I had to be prepared to let my old self die.

Do you want to change your life? I mean totally transform your habits and patterns, totally transcend your addiction – be it food, alcohol, sexual partners, drugs. Perhaps you want to get out of a toxic relationship, or move country? Then be willing to surrender everything you thought you knew up until this point; be willing to give it all up.

Everything that's the identity of 'you' consists of beliefs you have acquired about yourself and the world over the years: the environment you've spent your life in, cultural beliefs from your family and friends, and memories embedded in your subconscious, from your early childhood experiences until now. When you realize that all of that is just beliefs, then you realize you have the power to change those beliefs. How many times in your life have you believed one thing, then your perspective has changed and you've decided to believe something new instead? Loads. When you realize you have the power to choose your thoughts and choose your beliefs, you can completely transform your life. So what do you want to believe is true, and take on as truth? Ask yourself: *If I were to transcend this pattern/leave this relationship/change my life, what would I need to believe were true?*

Is your addiction solely to food? Then you would need to believe that your body was your best friend and was on your side. You would need to believe that recovery and healing was 100 per cent there for you, and that it had been there all along. You would need to believe that healthy food was delicious, exciting, nourishing and your favourite thing to put in your body. You would need to believe that working out is great fun, that those endorphins rock your world and that you're a better person for moving your body in a way that feels good.

If it's also alcohol, you would need to believe that you don't really need it to have a fun night out anyway; in fact, you find nowadays that you don't even crave it that much, and find it so much more rewarding to take better care of yourself. However, if you do want it, you have the power to choose it – at your discretion.

Are partners a problem? You would need to believe that you can fill your own cup, be the love of your own life and attract wonderful partners who treat you like a goddess – no exceptions. You would need to believe that there is no shortage of amazing partners in the world. They aren't all douchebags; there are some incredible partners out there waiting to love you – yes, *you* – in exactly the way you love yourself. You would need to believe that you are blessed and that miracles happen naturally for you, by default.

Want to quit your job? You would need to believe that the Universe has something much better in store for you, something that lights you up and makes you excited about Mondays. You would need to believe that the perfect next chapter is waiting for you when you take that leap. You would need to believe that you can achieve absolutely anything in this life – and that you really are absolutely limitless.

Every day we are choosing what we believe.

Whatever we believe to be true, is true – because we believe it to be so. So that becomes our truth. If you take on the belief that you will never heal your addiction, if you take on the belief that you will never fully get over your issues, if you take on the belief that it's in your genes to be overweight, or you always meet people who treat you badly – then that becomes your truth and you will continue only to see things that confirm that to be true. If you take on the belief that the world is unfair and full of pain – then guess what? It will be. Because that's all you'll see. Because you chose that story. Our beliefs become self-fulfilling prophecies.

Every day we are brainwashing ourselves with new thoughts and beliefs. When you realize you are the master of what you choose to believe, you can truly transform your life. Literally anything is possible.

Follow your freedom

When I first made that commitment to freedom around food – freedom in my own body, freedom from the scales and numbers – that's when I started unlocking freedom in other areas of my life: freedom in my relationships, freedom from people-pleasing, freedom in my business, freedom to travel, freedom to design and create my dream life.

When I continued to follow my freedom, it led me to everything that set my soul on fire. I started doing things that really lit me up. I started going to events I wanted to, seminars where I didn't know anyone else – all regardless of what other people would think. I released the guilt for spending time on myself. I did it because I felt something in my soul call me to do it.

And it felt like I was coming home to myself, even though externally I was still living in a world that didn't feel like mine. I was in a marriage that was breaking down, I was in a beautiful, perfect house that I felt completely trapped in, and I was in an area of the country that made me feel like a prisoner. But now I had learned to pay attention to that little voice, that nudge, that whisper. I started getting stronger and stronger. I started feeling freer and freer. I started feeling more and more at home within myself. And I started being me without needing anyone's permission. I got to know myself on a deeper level than ever before.

And I realized that when I did this, I was attracting towards me a whole network of like-minded people who I felt connected to. I met soul-sisters who I would keep in touch with. Every time I followed my soul's calling, it would lead me to something else that reinforced who I knew I was. And I felt like I was building my own self-confidence, my own sense of self. And my own tribe. I felt like I was finally finding out who I really was. I was building such a sense of inner freedom and self-worth, I was creating my own universe. And all of this had stemmed from my commitment to surrendering to self-love instead of to my eating disorder.

The more I empowered myself and became strong, the more obvious it became that I had to make a significant change if I wanted to be truly happy. My ex-husband and I were making each other miserable, and it wasn't fair on either of us that I pretended to be happy for any longer than I already had. I couldn't keep it up anymore. The whisper had turned into a scream. Each day I would pray for the strength and courage to leave. Until, on holding my first retreat in Turkey, something happened. I experienced such an incredible week with these women – they were my tribe, my soul sisters. I laughed, cried, and felt so connected and at home. I didn't miss my home in the UK, and I dreaded going back. I knew the time had come.

I had spent a long time following my freedom before I had even left for Turkey. I had spent a long time getting to know myself, getting to know *me*, and knowing for certain that if all else failed – I still had me. And that was good. I actually liked myself and my own company now. I knew I had my own back.

I had started to realize that when I had faith, worked hard and believed in myself, things would work out.

I knew that when I showed up as the woman I wanted to be, I would be supported. I knew that in order for me to grow, I had to be brave and fully commit.

Within a few days of arriving home, I calmly expressed that I wanted a divorce. I loved him, but I loved myself enough to know that this relationship wasn't healthy for me, and we both deserved better. A month later, after lots of crying and repeatedly questioning everything, I found myself driving away with nothing but a car full of stuff, wiping away floods of tears. It hurt – but it was right.

I moved into my mum's spare room with no plan whatsoever, but my soul was willing me on, every step of the way. I knew I was abandoning my old life, but I had an unwavering trust that I was being called to create something new that was truly from my heart.

After another solid month of crying into copious glasses of wine and watching episodes of *Sex and the City* (which I strongly believe is a crucial part of every divorce or break-up), I moved into a small flat in West London and started afresh. New city, new friends, a new life. I prioritized new experiences, travel and adventure. I looked after myself. I pursued my dreams wholeheartedly and unapologetically. And life got a hell of a lot better. By this time, my self-love game was so strong that even the crazy energy of London couldn't pull me down. I had truly conquered my demons around food, and it had led me on the most incredible journey.

I want to state that I am still a strong believer in the sanctity of marriage, but I believe that marriage isn't something that should be jumped into when you're 20 years old and infatuated, and don't really know who you are yet. Easy to say in hindsight, I know. But make sure it's the right person and you both have the same values, the same beliefs and the same vision for your future together.

Divorce is an ugly beast, a sort of grieving and emotional rollercoaster that goes on for a long time after the separation itself. It's like a death. You are grieving the partner you left behind, but also the dreams you built together, the memories, and your old self too. Because that girl is never coming back.

Divorce isn't something to take lightly. Truthfully, mine gave me the most pain I've ever known. When you've been in a relationship with someone from such a young age, it's hard to know who you are without them. I often questioned whether I lost parts of myself during the divorce or whether I lost them in the marriage. Either way, I was determined to find them again. Fast forward a few years and I can honestly say it was absolutely the best decision I could have made at the time.

It was never about food

My self-love journey all started with that one decision to pursue freedom from my destructive eating disorder and body patterns. Freedom from the struggles I was facing with food – because it was never really about food in the first place. It was about me suppressing who I really was and what I really wanted from life.

> **When someone is full up by their life,**
> **you don't often find them constantly**
> **turning to food to make them feel 'full'.**
> **That feeling of being satisfied, nourished,**
> **full, is not sustainable with food. It is**
> **we who must make ourselves full.**

Have you ever spent ages trying to feel 'full' from food, never allowing your body to speak to you, always filling your body with this food, that food, this meal, this snack – constantly chasing 'full up'?

If you are facing your own food struggles and demons right now, I invite you to ask yourself:

Is this really about food itself, or is this about me suppressing who I really am?

Is this really about sugar cravings, or is this a craving for something much deeper than that, something that food cannot give me, but that I must give to myself?

And, instead of trying to change your food habits, could you ask yourself:

How could I show up more fully as myself each day?

* Choose to believe your body is deserving of being healthy and fit. It's your natural state.

* Choose to believe you find taking care of your body easy and effortless – it's just part of who you are.

❧ Choose to believe you can have the job of your dreams – of course. Why settle for anything less?

❧ Choose to believe you can travel and see the world. Why not? It's out there waiting for you.

❧ Choose to believe there are tons of amazing partners out there, who know exactly how to treat a woman well, are emotionally available, great at communication and great in bed too.

❧ Choose to believe that love and beauty are everywhere you look.

❧ Choose to believe that you don't actually 'need' that wine every night. You choose it, as and when you want it.

❧ Choose to believe that you are a master creator – anything you imagine, you can make real.

❧ Choose to believe that we live in a beautiful, incredible world, full of love and compassion.

This isn't about pretending everything's rosy and wonderful if you're having a shit day and just want to cry into your pillow. That's completely allowed. It's not about glossing over the bad times and being positive all the time. That's a dangerous game and will have you suppressing your true emotions. No – this is about resetting your default belief system so that you naturally see the good. It makes you stronger, more grateful, more resilient and, to be honest, a more compassionate and loving human being, too.

This is how I now try to live my life, how I transcended my negative thoughts and feelings around food and my body, and how I began to create my dream life. It's how I transcended old, toxic relationships, stopped attracting the same type of guys and attracted real love instead. But first, I had to believe it was possible for love to show up for me in a different way than it had done.

I chose to believe I could create any life I imagined, because my imagination was the most powerful tool I had.

I chose to believe that full recovery from my eating disorder was already in motion. I believed myself into it. And before I knew it, I was looking back at it as an old version of myself. I began painting it into my past instead of my present. And it became the truth. I chose to believe it was possible and already happening, instead of keeping myself trapped in the fear and limitations of believing 'I can't' and 'poor me'.

Choose to see miracles and beauty everywhere, and you will. Choose to look for the beauty and purity in everyone (including yourself) rather than the flaws, and you will find them. Or you can live in a world where all you choose to see is pain and suffering. It's your call.

Our external world reflects our internal state. Transform your inner world, and your outer world will reflect back at you to match it.

Your food = your life

You may have heard the phrase, 'How you do anything is how you do everything.' This stems from the fact that everything you do in life is based upon the relationship you have with yourself.

This is why, when we start to dive into the relationship we have with food, it becomes clear that food was never really the issue in the first place. It becomes clear that there were elements of our lives that were unbalanced, out of alignment, and which were leading to us express ourselves with sabotaging patterns, using food – or lack of food – as our weapon of choice.

Just like our relationships with everything else – with our bodies, money, nature, time, other people – are all simply a reflection of our single main, most important relationship: the one we have with ourselves.

So how key is it to have a good relationship with yourself? Pretty crucial, I'd say. And what's more, your relationship with yourself is also what creates your relationship with life. Allow me to explain, because when I realized this, it blew my mind.

If you have a stressful relationship with food, you probably have a stressful relationship with life.

If you rush through your food quickly, always thinking about the next meal, you're probably someone who also rushes through your life pretty damn quickly, always thinking about the next thing.

If you're a perfectionist around food, it's likely you're a perfectionist in life.

If you're all-or-nothing with food and dieting, you're probably also all-or-nothing in your life.

If you're someone who loves breaking the rules of life and hates to conform, you probably have a pretty hard time sticking with diets.

If you don't feel nourished by your life, it's highly unlikely that you'll be feeling truly nourished by your food.

If you feel guilty about receiving pleasure in your life, you probably feel guilty for receiving pleasure from food.

If we struggle to slow down as eaters, we most likely struggle to slow down in life.

If we have chaotic rhythms around food, we most likely have chaotic rhythms around life.

If you're a control freak with your diet, you're probably also someone who highly values control in your life.

This is why simply going on a weight-loss diet will never address the reason for most people's unwanted and emotionally charged struggles around food – because it's not actually about the food itself. It's about your relationship with food, which equals…? Your relationship with *you* – and your relationship with your life.

> **Change your relationship with life, and the natural byproduct will be that you change your relationship with food.**

Relationship = everything

There's no denying that relationships are what's at the heart of life, what we all care about the most. They're also what all of us seem to also struggle with most. Why is it that the most important thing to us is something we find so difficult? Because we have simply not been taught.

Most of us spent years at school studying academic subjects, such as maths, English and science. A lot of time spent thinking with our minds – but how much time did we spend learning how to feel with our hearts? Most of us didn't spend a single hour in school on relationships, our emotions or how to love ourselves. We just had to pick it up as we went along, or copy our parents (who probably didn't get it right either) and hope we didn't mess up too much. Fortunately, to my delight, many of today's schools have started to add mindfulness lessons to their classrooms. It's a start. But when you and I were at school, that sort of education simply wasn't available. So is it any wonder we grew up confused about how to love ourselves, and that we continually mess up our relationships or end up in unhealthy ones? It's because *we haven't learned how to be in a relationship with ourselves.* Is it any wonder we grow up learning to bury our emotions in food or drink? Again, it's because *we haven't learned how to handle our emotions or to be with them, so our go-to is to numb them instead.*

Our relationship with ourselves determines everything in life.

Our relationship with ourselves determines how we connect with others.

It determines our relationship with our partner.

It determines our relationship with food.

It determines our relationship with our work.

It determines our relationship with our money.

It determines our relationship with the world.

It determines our relationship with time.

It determines our relationship with our Higher Power.

It determines our relationship with *everything*.

Have you noticed that the way we binge on food makes us feel the same as when we feel out of control when we're on a mad shopping splurge? Or that the way we control or restrict our food feels the same as when we control or restrict our spending?

If you're all-or-nothing with food, how likely is it that you're generally an all-or-nothing person in your life, in your work, in your finances, in your relationships? But when we heal our relationship with ourselves and begin to dive deeper into the truth of who we are and truly own our desires, all these aspects of our lives can transform. Similarly, if you dive into your relationship with food – or any of the above areas – you'll begin to heal your relationship with yourself. It's our relationship with ourselves that directly determines how we feel about the world, other people and our lives. You'll realize that all of your relationships improve because you have found a deeper connection within the relationship you have with yourself.

This is why self-love goes so much deeper than getting your nails done or taking bubble baths in the middle of the day. Yes, these things are a truly wonderful start (and I'm a huge fan of both), but do not underestimate self-love, for it is self-love – your relationship with yourself – that is key to transforming your entire life in front of your very eyes.

Questions to self

❖ *What am I now ready to surrender and let go of?*

❖ *Where am I craving more freedom in my life?*

❖ *When or with whom do I feel like I am suppressing who I really am?*

❖ *What patterns do I have around food right now?*

❖ *Where do I notice these same patterns show up in other areas of my life?*

❖ *What do I now choose to believe about myself and what is possible for me?*

Chapter 4

Soul
Cravings

*'All cravings are the mind seeking salvation
or fulfillment in external things and in the
future as a substitute for the joy of Being.'*

ECKHART TOLLE

What is it that keeps you up at night?

When you stop still and listen to yourself, what is it that you yearn for?

If you knew you couldn't fail, what would you do?

If you had one year left to live, what would you do with it? Where would you go? What desire would you finally own, and fulfil?

What would you break free from, if this were your only chance to do so?

What are you secretly yearning for that you have held yourself back from, for fear of what others will think?

What has your soul been longing to express?

What are your deepest desires, that you haven't even voiced out loud to your loved ones? Each of us has these desires, and try as we might to numb them, pretend they don't exist or brush over them, the more they build up. The more we suppress our deepest desires, the more we start to feel trapped by doing so. Our purpose is to express ourselves, to experience ourselves, to experience life – in all its beautiful, messy wonder. And when we deny our desires, we are slowly killing our soul.

This is also when food, alcohol or drugs temporarily become more important. They help us to numb our feelings. They help mask our pain. They help cover up the truth. But what if we were to condition ourselves to question everything, to investigate these behaviours, instead?

**Instead of focusing on what we're eating,
let's focus on what's eating us.**

What is a life without a story? Story is as intrinsic to us as food and breath are. Stories are what bind us as a people – we've been using them for centuries to connect with one another. And our own stories – the ones we tell ourselves about ourselves – become our lives, and become entwined with our identities. We tell ourselves the same stories over and over again until we believe them and recite them as gospel. And when the stories we've been telling ourselves are no longer believable to us, we have a breakdown and start to question everything. When our belief system is shattered, we have no chance but to rebuild.

When something bad happens to us that has happened to us many times before, we laugh and say, 'It's the story of my life!' We might say, 'I missed the train because I got the time wrong – the story of my life!' Or 'I just met the love of my life but he's moving to Africa on Monday – the story of my life!'

So, goddess, what's the story of your life? What's the story you're constantly playing out, over and over again? Maybe ask your friends what they think your story is. And why is it that we seem to get addicted to the stories that cause us pain or stress; addicted to the stories of it never working out for us?

It's because somewhere there's something that we unconsciously 'get' from it: a payout. It could be validation, pity or love from someone else. We get to play the victim. We have something to talk about. We get to have all the attention. It's our 'thing'. It's our story. We pretend we don't like it, but secretly there's a part of us that does. It feels safe to us – familiar and comforting.

Have you been the person who's constantly getting hurt by their partners, playing the same story over and over, with all of your friends rolling their eyes as you tell the story that this one – this one, who you said was different from the rest – turned out to be the same? I have.

Maybe dieting has become your story. Maybe it's become so intrinsically associated with your identity that you don't really know what to talk about if you're not talking about weight loss or what you did at the gym today.

Or maybe your busy-ness has become your story. Maybe every time someone messages you, all you can talk about is how busy and stressed you are, and how hard you're working all the goddamn time.

All three of these examples are stories I have at some point been addicted to myself. And the only way I was able to let go of these stories was to stop and listen to myself – and realize that, actually, I was sick and tired of my own bullshit. And I was ready to write myself a new story.

I had to take responsibility for the fact that it was me who was choosing to keep putting myself out there to get hurt. It was me who was choosing to live in the diet cycle and play that story on a loop. It was me who was choosing to allow work to stress me out and become a priority over family, friends and social life.

The stories we repeatedly tell ourselves are literally writing our futures.

A lot on my plate

Perhaps you're someone that carries 'busy' around like it's a prized trophy? We love to proudly revel in telling everyone how overworked and stressed out we are by our everyday lives, as if we'll get a medal, a nod of recognition or at least some degree of 'Wow, she never stops'; as if we're being utterly harassed by our own lives and never chose this for ourselves.

Could it be we are addicted to 'busy'? Addicted to our work, addicted to taking on more things and never stopping to come up for air? But could it really be that, rather than prizing ourselves on being such martyrs or competing for Best Businesswoman or Best and Busiest Mum on the Playground, we're actually just plain uncomfortable with the thought of our own stillness?

What would that feel like? To be… still? To say no. To delegate. To refuse tasks. To rip up the ever-growing to-do list? To just… be. By yourself.

What does that look like? Does it feel good? Maybe a touch awkward?

Why is it that in today's society we seem to have forgotten how to rest? And that we spend so much time 'doing', we forget about 'being'? Doesn't it seem that we're always trying to prove to someone (ourselves) how busy and important we are? How needed we are? How much of a high achiever and multitasker we are? We think it makes us some kind of a martyr to put everyone else before ourselves (mums, I'm looking at you), but in turn this creates the opposite effect, for when we can't even take care of ourselves, how can we possibly take care of others?

A stressful kind of lifestyle sees us also create stress around mealtimes. A stressful relationship with life equals a stressful relationship with food, and vice versa. And if you're anxious and worried about food, chances are you're anxious and worried about life in general.

What goes on in our psychology directly affects our physiology:

When you're upset (psychology), your eyes produce tears (physiology).

When you're anxious (psychology), your stomach goes into knots (physiology).

When you feel angry (psychology), you can often feel your heart racing (physiology).

And what happens when we feel stressed? Well, blood rushes to our heads and limbs, and away from our digestive system – meaning we're much less able to process and metabolize food.

Two mantras I often share with goddesses on my retreats are 'If I'm stressed, I won't digest' and 'I only eat when I am peaceful'.

Our bodies are directly affected by our emotions and our minds. But this isn't just brought on by real occurrences in life. It can also happen as a result of any imagined threat. You can imagine that a piece of chocolate cake is going to make you fat and unwell – but you can also sit down peacefully and eat the same piece of chocolate cake in a calm, relaxed state and believe it's an enjoyable, pleasurable experience. And you can get over it and move on with your life.

These two experiences will be completely different, both for you and for your body. The first will put your body into a state of stress, which means it will be unable to digest or assimilate the meal properly. The second will put your body into a peaceful, relaxed state – optimal for digestion.

This realization blew my mind, because so many times in the past I have sat down to eat and been completely stressed out by the whole experience. If I was eating carbohydrates, I would curse myself and call myself awful names the whole time I was eating, disgusted by the possible outcome from this meal and how much weight I would undoubtedly gain. And what I believed to be true, came true. My belly would puff out and swell up, and I would feel dreadful.

You may have heard of Japanese researcher Dr Masuru Emoto's experiments with water crystal experiment in the 1990s. He described his remarkable realization when he started *speaking to water*. When he spoke loving words of gratitude to the water then froze it, he claimed the crystals had transformed into beautiful shapes. When he spoke hateful words, the frozen water's crystals were 'disfigured'. Emoto believed that water was a blueprint for our reality, and concluded that human consciousness has a huge effect on the molecular structure of water.

What does this teach us? Our words, thoughts and actions can transform everything around us. When we speak lovingly and practise gratitude, everything can transform. And our bodies, our food *and the planet* are comprised primarily of… water.

When I made peace with food and was actually able to sit down and eat pasta in a calm, stress-free and loving state, I realized that the pasta was actually pretty delicious – and pretty harmless, too. I realized that when I ate it peacefully, I didn't bloat or notice too much difference at all. It was what I was making it mean that was doing the real damage.

Now, am I instructing you to live off pasta and chocolate cake just so long as you do it in a peaceful manner? Well, no. And I imagine doing this every day would not feel great for your body. Balance is key, and what's even more key is a healthy relationship with food. So don't take what I say as a solid instruction to live off a diet of peacefulness, pasta and chocolate cake. (If you're adamant on doing this of course, though, who am I to stop you?) My essential point here is that if you're living in a constant state of stress around your life – whether it's real or self-imposed – this will have a constant effect on your body and its ability to metabolize your food. Eating while peaceful is key and will help you digest everything you sit down to at the table.

So would you please:

Stop being such a maniac, woman.

Slow down and actually be still with yourself.

Eat your food only when you're in a peaceful state of mind.

When you sit down to eat, ask yourself, *Am I in a good mood right now?*

And break up with busy. Your kids won't love you any less. You won't suddenly become a slob. But you may find something you were hungry for all along.

If we want to change our stories and rewrite new ones, we first have to take responsibility and realize that we have created a lot of our own suffering from the stories we have chosen to believe as gospel. It is we who have continually chosen to replay those negative stories. And if a story isn't serving us any longer, or we decide that we're sick of it, we can choose to disassociate from that story and tell ourselves a new one instead. Only when we accept this can we get out of our victim mentality and choose to write something different for our lives.

Remember, you are writing your story. All the time. You're not just the author of the story, but the director, producer and in the starring role. You're the leading lady, not a supporting actor, not an extra. This is your story.

But are you playing the hero right now, or the victim?

Is your story one of pain, drama and things never quite working out for you? Or is it a story of overcoming obstacles, breaking the rules, finding love, and of adventures and self-discovery?

Social hierarchy is a sort of illusion that many of us spend our lives feeding into. This is the one that says: get good grades, get a job, climb the ladder at that job, meet a person, buy a house, get engaged, get married, have kids and so on. We go through life ticking all these boxes, largely because it's what we think we 'should' be doing. We think it's what our parents expect of us. We think it's what everyone else from school is doing. We don't want to get left behind. We need to keep up with everyone else, or stay ahead. But this is all an illusion, a game we're playing with ourselves, a story we've chosen to buy into. Social hierarchy consumes many people's lives and is the driving force for a lot of people doing... well, anything at all. It's a system that creates safety, structure, stability, conformity. But it's up to you if you want to go through life ticking boxes, or if you want to do things your own way.

So many people are so engulfed in what they believe others will think of them that they continue through life ticking box after box. They're always looking for the next box to tick, wondering why they don't actually feel fulfilled and why it always feels like something is missing.

Then what happens? They wake up one day and ask themselves, *Who am I? What do I actually want?* These people have been so engulfed by society's box-ticking that they've lost all sense of who they were to start with, before society told them who they should be. And as a result, not only do they feel deeply unfulfilled and disillusioned, but they also no longer believe that life can be any other way. They didn't follow their hearts, pursue their passions or what really lit them up as children. They did what their parents, or society, wanted them to do, then years later realized it was never truly in their hearts the whole, entire time. This is commonly known as a mid-life crisis, or nowadays – because people are waking up at a much younger age – a quarter-life crisis. Like the one I had.

Will you be someone who looks back at their life in years to come and asks themselves, *What the hell just happened to my life? Who am I, besides being a good parent or spouse, or being relatively good at my job? Who am I really here to be?*

The truth is that you, reading this right now, are very special. You are here for something more than ordinary.

Many people will continue through their lives playing inside the lines, never waking up to the truth of who they really are or what they're really here for, and never stepping out of their comfort zone. You, however, are different. You know there's more for you out there – and I know you're hungry for it.

Questions to self

❖ *What negative or damaging story have I been playing out over time?*

❖ *What am I ready to let go of?*

❖ *What do I choose as my new story instead?*

❖ *What does my soul crave, that I have been too scared to admit?*

❖ *When I'm by myself, I feel…*

❖ *Often, when I eat, I feel…*

Even with
nothing,
you are
enough.

Chapter 5

Feeding
the Void

*'Whatever you do, don't try and escape from
your pain, but be with it. Because the attempt
to escape from pain creates more pain.'*

SOGYAL RINPOCHE

Have you ever felt a sense that something is… missing? That there's a void inside you that needs to be filled somehow? That you're not quite… enough on your own? When you are alone with only you and your thoughts, does it feel uncomfortable, weird, unnerving? For me, it used to feel *a lot* uncomfortable and put me right on edge. It wouldn't be long before I'd turn to something to temporarily distract me from the bleak hole of nothingness. Usually, that was food. If it wasn't food, it would be social media or mindlessly texting someone. I couldn't be alone with myself or my thoughts for more than a few moments before it was too uncomfortable to bear, and I had to mask that pain with something that felt temporarily pleasurable. Pleasure isn't bad – it's beautiful. But it's powerful, and our relationship with it is often one that we can cleverly use to avoid our deeper cravings.

We live in a world that tempts us with all manner of addictions and most of us have, to varying degrees, let ourselves been sucked in, whether it's by food, alcohol, the Internet, other people, shopping, gambling. For some people, addiction shows up in a more obvious state – being addicted to cocaine or being dependent on alcohol every day. But for most of us it's a lot more subtle than that. We believe we'll feel better when we've eaten a Snickers bar. Or smoked a cigarette. Or had our third coffee. Or refreshed our Instagram feed, or gulped down a glass of wine, or bought those expensive shoes. We say, 'If I can just have X, then I'll be okay. Then I'll feel complete.'

The spiritual teacher Eckhart Tolle says, 'Every addiction starts with pain and ends with pain.' Comedian Russell Brand comes to the same conclusion in his book *Recovery*, where he describes the addictive cycle as starting with pain, leading to a distraction (the addiction) to numb the pain, then the negative effects of that distraction and the resulting shame – in other words, more pain.

Many of us find ourselves repeating this cycle, whether on a subtle basis or an obvious one. And, of course, this has been exploited in our materialist culture, because it's much easier to sell things to those who are addicted to them, especially if the media and advertising hit us from every angle: *When you have the latest iPhone, then you'll feel good about yourself; When you have this latest model of car, you'll finally feel like you've made it; When you download this dating app, then you'll meet The One and your life will finally be complete!*

When it comes to food, emotional eating and turning to food in times of stress or pain has become normalized by our society:

I'm sad. Have a chocolate bar.

I'm lonely. Text someone.

I'm bored. Get drunk.

More food to fill the void. More alcohol to numb the pain. More social media to send us further down into the rabbit hole of comparison and self-loathing. Sleep, wake up, repeat. And using food to deal with our emotions is so woven into our society that it's used time and time again in brands' clever marketing tactics, targeting our emotions head-on with their ads:

Have a break, have a KitKat. (Your life is tough, you need a break and you deserve to reward yourself with our chocolate biscuits!)

Coca-Cola. Life tastes good. (How great is life, you guys? Let's all celebrate our lives by drinking our carbonated sugary drink.)

Once you pop, you can't stop. (Normalizing eating a whole tube of Pringles in one sitting is not okay, Pringles.)

And arguably the worst culprit of them all, McDonald's with their 'Happy Meals', might as well say, 'Are your kids misbehaving again? Swing by and grab them a Happy Meal – that'll win them over. We've even thrown in their favourite collectable toy – what are the chances of that?' Yes, for many of us, by the age of six it was already imprinted onto our brains that food is a reward, a treat, and there to deal with our emotions and make us happy.

> **As we've grown up, many of us have proceeded to prioritize these things – food, alcohol, sex, drugs, material things – to the point where they become destructive.**

We sustain ourselves with distraction and momentary pleasure from them, until our lives become something of a blur because we're fixated on having that thing – whether it's a hamburger, 'that' dress, a drink at the end of the day or sex with that person who's unhealthy for us. So addicted are we to seeking happiness outside ourselves that we chase happiness around like a carrot on a stick: *When I lose 10 pounds, then I'm bound to be happier.*

And what happens? We go and do all of those things – we buy the car, we lose 10 pounds, we meet The One, we splash out on the dress, we lose another 10 pounds – and then we wonder why we're still not happy. We wonder what's missing. We wonder why that void still exists, why we still don't feel good enough.

We continue to chase happiness outside ourselves, but it's a never-ending cycle and a sad game that sucks true fulfilment out of anything. We are a society sick with 'Yes – but more!' and everything is done to excess. We can't stop at one biscuit, or one pay rise, or one drink. We need more and more – and then just a little bit more.

Like many of you, I've had my fair share of playing out such addictive patterns. And even after these years of healing and self-love, I still notice myself slip into them time and time again. This is the world we live in, and it's not something we should condemn or punish ourselves for doing. Although I don't do this with food anymore, I still notice that I sometimes crave a glass of wine to comfort myself if it's been a particularly stressful day. I notice that when I want to distract myself from something, I'll flick on my phone and start refreshing my social media feeds. The way that I've learned to overcome all of these habits, and continue to practise this, is simply by bringing a level of awareness to the habit. It's about recognizing that we are doing it but not judging ourselves, instead bringing some compassion and love to ourselves and then asking ourselves, *What is it I'm trying to get from this act?* It might be avoidance, comfort or reward. So, could you find comfort within yourself? Could you reward yourself with kind words of affirmation and praise to yourself, rather than using an external source to symbolize a win? And if it's avoidance or distraction, can you stop avoiding that thing and look straight at it, tackle it head-on? For this is where we will grow. This is how we will become our greatest versions.

Awareness is absolutely key. Reclaim your awareness. You are a human being with emotions, not a mindless zombie consumer. Become aware of your relationship with hunger and the reasons *why* you are turning to food. Before you eat, ask yourself, *Am I in a good mood? Am I avoiding something else?*

> **To actually satisfy our cravings, we must give ourselves what we are trying to get from an outside source like crisps, wine or another person. We must give ourselves what we need – not what we think we want. We must nurture ourselves, as a parent would a child.**

We must comfort and reward ourselves in healthy ways that nourish our soul. Sometimes when we think we want ice cream, what we really need is a big hug or an ugly cry. Sometimes, when we think we want to text that person who treats us badly, what we really need is to love ourselves more and stop seeking love from another.

If we don't recognize that happiness is an inside job, that this void can only be filled by ourselves, then, well, we're on course for a life of that same empty feeling, no matter how many boxes we tick or possessions we acquire. And when we don't feel fulfilled by the things in our life that are supposed to bring us happiness, we kid ourselves that we just haven't had enough of it, so we just keep seeking more.

Addiction: the root cause

'The real question in addiction is not "Why the addiction?" but "Why the pain?"'

GABOR MATÉ

Whatever our addiction – to food, to weight watching, to exercise, drugs or alcohol – how does this really happen in the first place? And is there ever a way to break free from it, or is this, perhaps, the curse of having an 'addictive personality'?

The author Johann Hari came up with a fascinating answer when he researched his book about drug addiction, *Chasing the Scream*. In an article for HuffPost about his research, Hari describes how he concluded that regular drug users were able to give up quite easily – when, ultimately, they were happier.

Amongst a number of examples he cites in his article are the 1970s experiments on rats that had become addicted to drugged water when in isolation with nothing else to do, but preferred plain water once they were in a cage with plenty of other rats and ratty apparatus to play on; he also refers to a study that found that of the 20 per cent of US soldiers who become addicted to heroin while fighting in Vietnam, most gave up as soon as they got back to their families; hospital patients given diamorphine – essentially a strong version of heroin, and often used for pain relief – show no need for it once they are home again. He also reported on the results of Portugal's ground-breaking response to its severe heroin problem: rather than putting drug users in jail, he explains how the country decriminalized drugs and used the unspent jail budget 'on reconnecting them – to their own feelings and to wider society'. They were given jobs and somewhere to live, making their life worth living for its own sake. The result was a 50 per cent reduction in drug use.

Hari's general conclusion from this and his other research is that human beings need connection – with themselves, with others, with the world. He says, 'The opposite of addiction is not sobriety. It is human connection.'

In summing up the results of the rat tests, he says, 'While all the rats who were alone and unhappy became heavy users, none of the rats who had a happy environment did.' Of course, humans live much more complex lives than rats, and life is constantly throwing us curve balls, but that happy environment can just as easily refer to human beings – not necessarily their home environment and living circumstances, but their true happiness, their inner world, since it's our inner world that so often dictates what shows up in our external world.

And when I think back, I can see that Hari's findings are completely relevant to my own addictions. I was unhappy in my cage when I developed an eating disorder. I felt overwhelmed, out of my depth, disconnected from the world and alone in my environment.

> **If I'd felt happy, connected and nourished by my relationships, and generally content, my eating disorder would arguably not have formed at all.**

In 2017 Russell Brand reached a milestone, having been free from drugs and alcohol for 15 years, thanks to the famous 12-step programme for recovering addicts, originally devised by Alcoholics Anonymous. The programme is widely used for alcoholics, drug addicts, sex addicts and various other addictions, and it has an incredible success rate. Why? Well, although at first glance some 12-step programmes can seem outdated and full of religious dogma, they give addicts what they were truly hungry for all along: connection. They provide a way for addicts to surrender to a power greater than themselves and to finally find purpose and deeper meaning in life. And it works.

In his book *Recovery*, Brand says his reasons for addiction started when he was a child. 'The impulse that made me eat too much chocolate when I was a kid was the same impulse that led me to heroin addiction in a child-friendly, socially acceptable disguise… I was using external resources to medicate because I felt uneasy inside.'

He also traces his battle with alcohol back to his childhood, recalling during a television interview with Oprah Winfrey that, '[As] a little kid I felt very lonely, isolated and confused, and anything that could temporarily relieve that, I was very grateful for.'

> **It is not the food or the substance but our relationship with it, which stems from an unhealthy relationship with ourselves or an unhappy environment we find ourselves in.**

So, when we open the fridge, looking for answers, what are we really trying to feed? If that void we sensed was already full, from our own happiness, would we even need to do that?

My answer is no. When we open up our social media for another hit, what is it we're really seeking? I personally notice that when I am fulfilled and happy with the company I am in, and with my environment, I am far less likely to pick up my phone, because I feel a deeper sense of connection.

What are you avoiding?

When addictive behaviour shows up, often they point to us avoiding some uncomfortable situation we don't want to deal with: words gone unsaid with your partner, a looming deadline at work, an issue you don't want to deal with.

Or maybe, just maybe, you're avoiding your bigger purpose. Maybe you're ignoring all the warning signs that your life is out of alignment and that actually, something needs to shift. These patterns and habits don't just show up willy-nilly, you know. They all have a purpose. They all have a meaning. They're there for a reason. Ask yourself, *What's up with this? What am I avoiding looking at here? Where is this habit coming from? What is this in response to?* And follow the stepping stones to where these questions take you.

Remember, finishing that pack of cookies won't make your problems go away. Blowing £20 at Marks and Spencer on fancy sandwiches when you aren't even hungry won't make the conversation with your boss any easier. And drinking all that wine won't make the bills pay themselves, kiddo.

Remember – what we resist persists.

Sometimes you need to give yourself a little kick in the tush and get real about what you're pretending not to see in your life that needs addressing. Give yourself a pep talk. For example:

Mel, I know you're trying to avoid finishing this project, but the time will pass anyway. Get off Instagram and... Do. The. Work.

Mel, I know you're doing all you can to avoid replying to that email, but the bottom of the cookie jar won't write the email for you. C'mon, girl.

Like so.

Put on your big-girl pants and deal with the real situation that's on your mind, however uncomfortable it may be, head-on. Self-love isn't about coddling yourself all the time and hoping the pain will just go away. Self-love is about giving yourself what you need in that moment. And sometimes, self-love is about looking that pain square in the eye and saying, 'I see what you are', and then being with that feeling, being with the entirety of that situation and accepting it for what it is. Have the awkward conversation. Finish the project. Call your mother. Only when you step out of your comfort zone will you grow. So what if shit feels uncomfortable? Good. You're moving forward. Next time, it won't be so hard.

Relax – nothing is under control

We are living in a world where only one thing is constant – change. Every day, this planet is evolving and growing and changing. Every day, people are evolving and growing and changing. Are you the same person you were a year ago? I sure hope not. If we aren't changing, we aren't growing. When flowers stop growing, they die. This is why any time someone says to you, 'You've changed...', I hope your response is, 'Good! I'd bloody well hope so!'

***We get this one precious shot at human
life. Do you really want to stay the
same your whole life, never growing
or expanding into anything new?***

It's impossible. Impossible for us not to change as a result of how the world is changing around us. So we may as well embrace it.

Look how much this planet has changed since you were a kid. We're living in the most incredible time Earth has experienced to date. We have limitless potential available, literally at our fingertips, more freedom than we've ever had, and with one click we can create or have anything we want in life. Ten years ago we were living in a totally different world, five years ago we were living in a totally different world, even one year ago! Look at how much has changed – on a personal level, on a technological level, on a global level.

Who were you five, 10 years ago? I'll bet you've grown and changed an awful lot since then. You aren't the same person. None of us is. Every single day, new beliefs are formed, perspectives are shifted, inventions are created, new relationships are made, and every time you return to a place, things are different. Every year, a new iPhone is released that go one step further than you could have thought possible. TVs are out, YouTube is in. Movies are out, Netflix is in. Radios are out, podcasts are in. Myspace was in, then Myspace was out and Facebook was in. Now Facebook is out and Instagram is in. Soon it will be something else.

And social media and technology is just the start. Most of us now can't watch TV without scrolling our phones at the same time; soon, cars will drive themselves, and we'll be able to scroll in the driver's seat. Before long, we'll all be able to hop on planes as if they're buses.

Still, as much as we can all debate the future of virtual reality, artificial intelligence and intergalactic space travel, we can't really predict what will happen or how it will happen. We don't know what our life is going to be like in one year, five years, 10 years from now. We don't know what's around the corner for us, our family, our friends. We don't know what path our careers will take, how our health will progress, what our children will grow up to be. We don't even know how we'll be spending our next birthday, or if we'll meet someone tomorrow who radically changes the course of our lives. We are living in a world that is unpredictable; that is full of uncertainty, mystery and constant change. This is the way of the Universe. This is the way it has always been.

We aren't in control of anything, even if we often pretend we are.

Yet most eating disorders and food issues stem from a conscious or subconscious desire to control our environment. It's never about the food itself, but about feeling in control in a world that is impossible to control – including, we believe, the issues we are avoiding. So we look to control the easiest, most available thing possible: food – or our weight, how our bodies look. But we can quickly wind up feeling out of control because in trying to rigidly control our food and our weight, we have instead given it enormous power – so it ends up being what controls us.

So rather than seeking to control an uncontrollable world, why not embrace the journey that is unknown?

Try relaxing into the beautiful flow and unpredictable nature of life.

Try living with uncertainty.

Try leaning into not knowing what's around the corner.

Try relaxing into realizing that nobody has all of the answers.

Try relaxing into realizing you will never be able to control everything, even food.

Try recognizing that the more you seek to control something, the more this will lead to feeling out of control.

Try relaxing into not knowing, or caring, what your weight is.

Try trusting that you don't have to control things in order to feel whole and complete. (In fact, it is the very action of doing this that is making you feel incomplete!)

Try relaxing into the certainty of change, and find comfort in the fact that our bodies are changing every single day, just as we are.

Try accepting that to attempt to keep our bodies at the same, controlled weight forever is simply impossible, and goes against the ways of the Universe.

Your body isn't the same as it was yesterday, a year ago, or five years ago. Neither are you. This is why, when you start to heal your relationship with food, it can often transcend into a deeper, more spiritual practice. It's about trusting that you don't have to try to control everything anymore. It's about relaxing into knowing that you're part of something greater at play. And having faith and believing in guidance from a power higher than yourself. And recognizing that, actually, in trying to control everything, you are holding yourself back from experiencing many miracles that come from the unknown.

> *When we release the need to control, we remember how to be free. When we relax and allow ourselves to trust that we are safe in our bodies, we can also relax and allow ourselves to trust that we are safe, and held by the Universe.*

The scarcity mindset

The so-called scarcity mindset refers to the way that, as a culture, we are never satisfied, and why we tend to often think in terms of 'never enough': never good enough, never successful enough, never thin enough, never enough time, never enough money, never enough sleep, never enough love. Basically, no matter what we have and how much of it we get, it's just... Never. Enough.

In today's culture, we are highly aware of what we don't have enough of. This is perpetuated by the average 400–600 images we each see on social media every day, selling us what we don't have and telling us what we don't look like. We look to our social feeds and are told, 'Have this – then you'll be good enough or feel better about yourself for a short, fleeting moment', which keeps us striving for more, hooked on the illusion of perfection while looking around at what everyone else has, thinking everyone else has got it better than we have.

It is this scarcity mentality that keeps us stuck from growing; the feeling of never having, or being, enough, makes us play the same story over and over, and instead of living in trust, we live in fear and doubt. This shows up time and time again for women, because we become convinced that we're all competing against each other to be 'beautiful', 'lovable' and 'sexy', and that there is only a certain amount of each to go around.

Diet culture perpetuates the scarcity mentality in a big way.

When there is something that we want, but are afraid we can't have, we want it even more. Regardless of how much food is available, dieting leads to us feeling like there is a food scarcity or the food will run out if we don't eat it all quickly enough. Have you ever eaten all of the food in your house on a Sunday night, telling yourself, *I'd better eat while I can, because once I go back on my diet, I'll stay on it forever, and who knows when I'll have the chance again?* Me too. The knowledge that you can't – or rather, the feeling that you shouldn't – eat what you want to eat will always lead to you feeling deprived.

And when you do finally allow yourself the chance to have a 'forbidden' food, it's never enough to have just *some*. Once you give in, the floodgates are open and you just can't stop eating – because you've been restricting yourself. You think food will suddenly vanish (or you won't be 'allowed' it again), so you'd better make up for it by eating it all right now. It's a sense of 'Have it now, because this is the last chance you'll ever have, because you'll be so strict later!' It's the same mindset that tells us we aren't good enough, that time is running out and that we'll never be able to afford the things we want in life.

This scarcity mindset is woven into our society, so how do we get out of the trap of scarcity thinking? By tapping into an abundance mindset instead. Having an abundance mindset is about believing that there's already more than enough for everyone, and knowing that we are provided with absolutely everything we need in any given moment – with food, with money, with time, with everything. It's about seeing what we do have, instead of focusing on what we don't. Remember this well-known saying: 'The secret to having it all is believing you already do.'

Stephen R. Covey describes the difference between scarcity and abundance mindsets in his book *The 7 Habits of Highly Effective People*:

> *'Most people see life as if there were only one pie out there. And if someone else were to get a big piece of the pie, it would mean less for everybody else. The Abundance Mentality, on the other hand, flows out of a deep inner sense of personal worth and security. It is the paradigm that there is plenty out there and enough to spare for everybody… It opens possibilities, options, alternatives, and creativity.'*

If you really wanted to, you could eat ice cream every day of the week. But if you tune in to your body, you'll find it won't actually like the idea of that. The only reason you have thoughts of eating ice cream every day is because you've been living with scarcity, believing that ice cream is forbidden and you are only allowed it on special occasions or when you deem yourself worthy. When you relax into abundance and realize that you hold the key to this mindset, you realize that you are the one who decides how to see the world. Would you like to see it through the scarcity lens, or the abundance lens?

Remind yourself that:

* There is plenty more where that came from.

* There is plenty for everyone to have enough – including you.

* There are always more opportunities for the Universe to provide you with exactly what you want.

We often tell ourselves, 'Something's gotta give!' and that when one thing goes well in our life, *Typical – something else goes to shit! You can't have it all!* If this is the story you want to keep telling yourself, then honey, play on. But I want to offer you a different story. I'm here to tell you that you *can* have it all. You just need to believe that you deserve to.

You can have everything you ever dreamed of in your life – all at the same time, too! If you can get your mindset to truly believe that this is possible for you, and you are worthy, then you can create it in your reality. But if you want to keep believing that you can enjoy only one thing at a time, then that's exactly what you'll end up with. It's your call.

In order to get over our scarcity mentality, we must feel safe in the knowledge that we will always have enough – and that the Universe is supporting us in abundance. And remember, there is plenty more where that came from.

Questions to self

* *Where has addiction shown up in my life before, and where is it now?*

* *What vices do I tend to turn to first, when I feel uncomfortable, uneasy or emotional?*

- *What am I avoiding or resisting right now?*

- *Where in my life am I constantly trying to control something?*

- *Where has scarcity thinking been showing up in my life?*

- *Does my environment support me? What could I do, to create a happier, more nurturing environment for myself?*

Chapter 6

Hungry for Change

'If you believe it will work out, you will see opportunities. If you believe it won't, you will see obstacles.'

Dr Wayne Dyer

When I think back to all the times my food patterns were particularly destructive or unhealthy, I can always see that in actual fact, no, I wasn't really hungry for a pack of Oreos or a £20 bag of pick 'n' mix. I was hungry for drastic change in my life. I wasn't happy with where I was. Maybe I didn't know exactly what I wanted to change, but I knew I wanted something different from what was my current situation. Perhaps it was a more fulfilling job or a relationship with someone who understood me; it might have been more girlfriends, a different location, more freedom; it could have been more fun, more pleasure; or more opportunities for creative expression. Just a change. I was bored and frustrated. I felt like I was standing still and not growing. I was really hungry for a change.

Kerry is a client of mine, a working mum-of-three from Bicester. By society's standards, she had ticked all the boxes and done everything right. She had her degree, her post-graduate qualification and had not just three but 11 letters after her name – yes, 11. She'd worked excessively long hours for most of her working life and taken jobs she didn't like, just to climb the corporate ladder. 'I had set myself the goal to be a Head of HR in a FTSE 100 company by the age of 35, and I had achieved it, with a few months to spare! With each new promotion, pay rise and added level of responsibility, I thought I would be happy. I kept telling myself, *If I can just get there, it will all have been worth it*. But it never was.' She also revealed she felt completely empty and unfulfilled in her work.

To numb the pain, Kerry turned to food. Dieting, weighing and the scales became the distraction technique to avoid looking at the pain or admitting she needed to change her situation. Food became everything – a punishment, a reward, a best friend, a worst enemy. "I always had another 7 pounds to lose, and no matter how many diets I did I could never get to my goal weight – and hated myself for it."

Kerry joined my programme, The Academy, to heal her relationship with food and her body, and it became clear straight away that the root of her situation had nothing to do with food. Sure, food and dieting had become the symptom, but it was her unfulfilling job that was the actual problem. She was hungry for change in her life.

Fast-forward a year and Kerry has not only healed her food issues, but figured out what she was hungry for – more satisfaction from her work, and more fulfillment in general. She has now dropped the need to tick boxes and is doing work that makes her soul happy. She decided she wanted to help other women stuck in unfulfilling jobs to start taking better care of themselves and now runs her own private health consultancy practice. 'I'm now days away from launching my first programme,' she said joyfully, 'and sometimes I still can't believe that I get to do a job that I love while also having the flexibility to be the mummy that I want to be. I always thought it was only other people who could do a job they love – but now that's me!'

After spending 35 years ticking boxes, she realized it didn't light her up. It didn't make her happy, and it was the root of her emotional eating, chronic dieting and self-loathing. But when she found the courage to make the change, everything began to click into place. And with a fulfilled life and a boost of energy, there's no longer the need to fill the hole in her life with food or dieting.

Abi is another young goddess I work with who told me she had always dreamed of studying psychology and helping others, but when her eating disorder took over her life she was unable to get the grades she needed. Instead of following her dreams, she took a route her parents suggested and wound up studying business and marketing for four years. She graduated and got herself a digital marketing job, but knew deep down it wasn't her calling in life. She said, 'Every aspect of my life had become this mismatched puzzle of life choices based on what other people wanted for me, rather than being true to myself.'

When Abi began the programme, she came in to heal her relationship with food and hoping to find a way out of her eating disorder. Not only did she do this but, better still, she gained a new-found freedom and confidence that enabled her to create the space to rediscover and pursue her true passions. She has now begun to retrain, in psychotherapy and counselling, so she can create the future she had always dreamed of. 'It was an opportunity to look into myself and understand myself, which gave me the confidence to finally build the life I want – not the one my mum, grandparents or friends want, but me!'

If either of these stories resonate with you and alarm bells are going off in your head right now, then girl, take back your life. You are only one decision away from completely changing it. If you suspect that you're hungry for change, and your relationship with food could be pointing towards you taking a big leap or pivoting 180 degrees, then buckle up. It's not going to be easy, but it's going to be worth it. Because the world needs your light. Yes, I'm talking to you.

If you have a gift that you're not sharing with the world, a passion you're not pursuing, a truth you're not speaking, a topic you're fascinated with but not learning about, you're doing a disservice to the rest of us.

The world needs you to shine your light, girl.

And when you shine your light, it gives others permission to do the same.

Don't let life pass you by, doing a job that sucks the soul out of you only because your dad wanted you to become a doctor when you really wanted to become a chef. Life is just too short for that shit. The world needs more people doing what they love and following their hearts. When you do something that sets your soul on fire, the world instantly becomes a more beautiful place to live in. Why, for heaven's sake, are you trying to fit in when you were born to stand out? Do something radical. Make a bold move. Take a leap of faith, and the Universe will catch you.

We all have a voice and now, thanks to the Internet and technology, we literally all have a platform to share messages that really matter to us and to express ourselves however we please. It's time for you to speak your truth and be who you were put here to be. You have a platform. Your voice matters – use it. Express your damn self, whether that means changing careers, starting a side gig or telling your partner that it's over. Be you. Life is too short not to.

You can be the change. *Yes, you.*

If you are reading this and nodding along but thinking, *Ok Mel, I know I'm hungry for change, but I'm just not sure what, or how*, then I hope the journaling prompts here will be of help to you. Grab a pen.

Questions to self

* *Where in my life do I feel unsatisfied or unfulfilled?*

* *What is currently not working?*

* *What is a big change I could make in this area?*

* *What feelings come up for me when I think about this change?*

* *What do I feel myself wanting to turn to when these feelings come up?*

* *What scares me most about making this change? Who am I afraid of upsetting?*

* *What do I need to let go of, in order to make this change?*

* *What action step can I take this month to initiate this change?*

Intuitive eating paves the way for intuitive living.

Chapter 7

An Appetite for Life

'Life will give you whatever experience is the most helpful for the evolution of your consciousness.'

ECKHART TOLLE

These are the steps and tools I have used, and continue to refer to, whenever I've wanted to create change in my life, get over fears and walk boldly towards a new future for myself:

1. Live in a state of gratitude

Gratitude comes first. Before you make a big change, get into a state of gratitude for everything you have right now, even if you plan to leave it behind. Before you walk away, be absolutely certain that you have given this your best go. That way you will never think back and say you could have tried harder. Write down all the reasons you're grateful for that comfort zone, that job, that person, that city, that thing. Whatever it is, thank the Universe for sending it your way and for allowing it to keep you safe and be your comfort zone for a while. Recognize all the ways it has helped you, served you, made you the person you are today. Bask in this gratitude awhile. If it's a person, see them in their most loving, natural state. If it's a job, remind yourself of how happy it made you when you began. If it's a place, see the parts that bring back the best memories. Love it. Thank it.

Appreciate it.

And then lovingly say goodbye.

2. Lock in your vision

Get clear on exactly what you want. Be as specific as possible. Write it down every day. Tell someone about it – this makes it more real and makes you really step up your game. Taste it. Smell it. Hear it. Touch it. Feel it. See it. Experience all of it. Meditate on it often. Visualize it every day.

> **Make your vision as real as possible. This is where your reality is first created.**

3. Make space

Declutter and create space in your life for what it is you want to come into your reality. If you want to go away on an adventure, book out the time in your calendar now. If you want to meet The One, you need to end the sucky relationship you're in just because you're lonely and passing the time. If you want to land your dream job, can you create more space for it to come in – make moves to quit your current job, get things in place, line things up? Could you quit now; send an email? Could you do it? Make space for what you really want. Act as if everything is already on its way to you.

4. Shift your identity

Instead on focusing on what you need to do, ask yourself, Who is the person I need to become to pull this off? What does that person choose to believe? Affirm to yourself:

I choose to believe I am worthy.

I choose to believe I am enough.

I choose to believe I can do anything I put my mind to.

I choose to believe I can do this.

I choose to believe the Universe has my back.

In order to become someone new, you must first make peace with your past – forgive it, and be willing to let your old self die. Again, bask in a state of gratitude for that girl. She was doing her best with the tools she'd been given. She kept you safe for a long time. Love her. Forgive her. Thank her.

And now let her go. The new you is waiting to be reborn.

To shift your identity, decide to no longer associate with how you used to behave, how you used to respond to certain scenarios. Your past has served you, it is a part of you by all means, but if particular habits, beliefs and patterns no longer serve you, then you require a change. Get clear on the woman you want to become. How does she think, feel, act, behave? What are her habits and her daily, weekly rituals? How does she live and spend her time? What is her belief system? Get to know her – Your Future Self – really well, like she's your best friend. Know everything about her. Your Future Self is the vision of yourself that you hold, and this vision is unbelievably important when it comes to making big changes in your life. Collect images and ideas that make up Your Future Self's life and add them to the big picture. Write Your Future Self letters often; talk to her.

Ask Your Future Self for advice often, and she will guide you to where you want to be.

She is, of course, your existing self – but she is the self you've been hiding all this time. She is the self you're destined to become. You are creating her, but you are also revealing her. She is the powerful you, who knows her worth. She is who you have been all along. When old beliefs come up, reject them and associate them with your past self, not Your Future Self. Act as if everything is already on its way to you. Live inside your vision.

5. Stare your fear in the face

When you make a commitment to yourself, the Universe will test you. Resistance will come up. Your comfort zone will begin to look extra cosy. Maybe your boss will offer you a pay rise to stay, or your partner will promise for the gazillionth time that if you continue with the relationship, something big will change. Your commitment to yourself will be tested almost straight away. The Universe is saying, 'Are you sure you wanna commit to that? Here's something to test you.'

Make sure you're sure. Stare your resistance in the eye. Notice where you are procrastinating. Notice where you are trying to be a perfectionist. Notice where you are pretending not to look. Notice what you are pretending not to see. When these tests have come up for me, my favourite way to deal with them is to notice them, laugh to myself and say, *How funny that this has come up, as soon as I've made a commitment! Old me would have totally done (enter old habit here), but new me is going to choose the opposite.* Choose for Your Future Self, not for your past self.

6. Take massive aligned action

This is key, key, key. Don't just have the vision and take no action. With that strong vision you now have, based on the previous steps, take massive aligned action in the direction of your dreams and The Future You. Create an action plan, step by step. What do you need to physically do next to make everything possible? Make bold moves. The Universe (which is you) responds to this in big ways. Live inside your vision. Keep checking in with The Future You – what must you do to become her? Keep taking aligned action steps. Book the ticket. Send the email. Build the website. Sign the papers. Create the programme. Research and plan everything. Then do it.

Don't wait around. You're ready.

Kasia is a goddess I've worked with for a little while, and she has the most infectious, bad-ass energy. When Kasia decides something, she does it. When I asked her if she had any words to add to this chapter of the book, she said, '"I don't even recognize myself" – they're words you usually use to describe a version of yourself you see and don't like, but in this case, "I don't recognize myself" is a good thing. One year into my journey with Mel's Academy and this is how I feel.'

Kasia explains what's changed. 'Today I'm a passionate, vibrant and beautiful woman – but that wasn't the me I'd settled for just a few short months ago. I've quit a job that was literally sucking the soul out of me, with no other job but a conviction that this is what would serve me. I've moved back to a place that fills me with joy. I've given up diets, my scales, negative thinking and a need for validation from others. I've started a new career and I bloody love it. I'm seriously exploring my love of photography. I've started writing a book – wow, that's been my secret dream since I was a teenager!'

There are fundamental changes, too, she says. 'I have a deeper spiritual connection with the Universe and with myself. I'm full of gratitude and awe. I've met some of the most inspiring and wonderful women that the Earth has been blessed with and I'm lucky enough to count many of them as lifelong friends. Oh – and I fell in love too. With myself.'

Imagine if women put more effort into shaping the world than they put into changing their shape.

Chapter 8

Hungry for
a Mission

'If you can't figure out your purpose, find out your passion. For your passion will lead you right into your purpose.'

BISHOP T.D. JAKES

Are you a woman on a mission, or are you void of a mission right now?

Because many of us got a little lost along the way, didn't we? Tainted by diet culture and media manipulation, we somehow became convinced that our mission in life was to change our bodies. We somehow became convinced that our value was all but a number. So that we knew where we fitted in. So that we knew our place. So that we could label ourselves as 'good'. Like cattle in line for the slaughter, with numbers painted onto our bodies: 142, 178, 180 – as if a number is all that defines us.

This number should be like the other numbers in your life that don't define you – your height, your date of birth or your passport number – and over which you have no control. But this number has somehow claimed a different role. We have allowed it to determine our mood, our relationships, our self-esteem. We lose ourselves in it and we forget everything else.

When did your mission become solely to change a number on the scale?

Instead of Jayne Atkinson, CEO, loving mum of three girls and passionate about saving the whales, we become Jayne: CW 150, GW 120.

Instead of Marie Carpenter, talented artist, jazz-lover and champion baker, we become @slimmingmarie123.

Instead of Rachel Williams, animal rights activist, fashion junkie and professional wedding planner, we became @racetobethin.

Our identities get buried, swallowed whole by diet culture. We forgot about who we were, believing that only when we drop our numbers sufficiently would we be granted a full, enriched life.

How dare you?

How dare you not realize your own power?

How dare you believe that God put you on this planet solely to shrink yourself?

How dare you believe this is the only reason you are here?

Enough, woman.

Enough playing small.

Enough underestimating your potential.

Enough being on hold as your life passes before your eyes.

I see you.

I see a powerful woman, capable of changing the world.

I see a woman who knows her own strengths, who follows her passions, who knows who she came here to be.

When powerful women join hands, I see a new world, a new age.

> *I see a world where women are free.*
> *They know what they came here for.*
> *They know who they are here to be.*
> *No longer are they here to fit into a dress or*
> *to change the backs of their thighs.*
> *No, these women are not wasting time*
> *on meaningless pursuits.*
> *They know their worth.*
> *They know they've got important shit to do.*
> *They know they aren't here to change their bodies.*
> *No.*
> *They're here to change the world.*

Adventure
begins
the moment
you decide
to say YES.

Chapter 9

Hungry for Adventure

'Life is an adventure. It's not a package tour.'
Eckhart Tolle

As a teen, I couldn't for the life of me understand why someone would grow up in one city and stay there for their entire lives. I grew up in Coventry, but knew I didn't fit into this city. To me, it was boring, dull and there was nothing exciting to do. Why on Earth would someone stay in that city when there was an entire world out there waiting to be explored?

For years I had a photo of somewhere in Bali, set as my computer's screensaver. It looked like somewhere magical, enchanted. One day, I hoped, maybe I would get to go there – or even get to run a retreat there for the women I had started to work with. I told a few people this dream and they laughed at me. But a seed had been planted and I locked in my vision.

Travelling had always been something I'd loved – ever since I was a child I've treasured the magic of travel. I would always dream of faraway lands and cultures yet to be explored, and swoon over paradise-island photos. However, when you live with disordered eating, the reality is that travelling can feel like a living hell, as you've no control over what food you're eating and your routines go completely out the window. The ability to travel has, for me, been a huge reward and accomplishment since healing my relationship with food. I've discovered that surrendering and letting go of control enough to get on a plane, totally alone, and spend time in a country you've never before been to, is an incredible adventure and will teach you more about yourself than any book or teacher will.

Travel for me is what lights my soul on fire; it nourishes me in so many ways, educates me, nurtures me and forces me to grow. After I left my old life behind, it wasn't long before I was jumping on a plane. A solo adventure was exactly what I needed. I just wanted to get away. Truthfully, I didn't know if I was running away from myself or towards myself. All I knew was that I was running. I needed some time by myself, away from England. I needed sunshine. I needed space. Something in me knew that this wasn't the right time for Bali. So I decided I would go to New York for the first time, then on to Los Angeles. Six weeks would do the job. And I was going alone.

This trip was wild. I felt like a bird that had just been let out of its cage for the first time in 25 years. It was worlds away from Coventry. I couldn't stay still. I rented a flat in Lower East Side, but I barely stayed indoors for more than a few hours, or just to sleep at night. I spent every day adventuring by myself, wandering the streets, making friends, sitting in cafés, opening my laptop everywhere to write, then exploring the restaurants and cocktail bars at night. Then, in Los Angeles, I soaked up the California sunshine, hiked in the canyons and took long road trips to Big Sur and Palm Springs with friends. It was just what the doctor ordered.

When I landed home in England, I felt rejuvenated and excited by life. My past hadn't gone away, but satisfying my cravings for travel and adventure had allowed me to see things from a new perspective. I came back fresh-faced, revitalized and feeling ready to take on the world.

A few months later, I randomly found myself at a kind of country show and exhibition. Equestrian activities and all kinds of market stands were on display. One stand in particular grabbed my attention. It was full of plaques, statues and gigantic Buddha faces, carved from wood and beautifully painted. A giant Buddha plaque caught my eye and I was determined to buy it for my new flat.

A friendly, older man with a thick cockney accent came up to me and within seconds was convincing me I'd made a wonderful choice and the Buddha had to be mine. This man was George. George told me all about his business and what had brought him along to the fair that day to sell his wares. 'Let me tell you something about this Buddha,' he said. 'This Buddha was hand-carved in Bali.'

My eyes nearly popped out of their sockets. 'Bali?' I gushed, 'I've always dreamed of going to Bali.'

As it turned out, not only had George lived in Bali for 15 years, but he had a beautiful Indonesian wife and children in Bali too, who I would later meet. He also happened to own a series of big villas there, which he said would be perfect for my first Bali retreat. He invited me to come out to Bali to stay with his family, check out the villas and see if they would be suitable.

The Universe had delivered me the opportunity to grab my dream with both hands.

Within days I had booked my flights. I didn't need anyone's permission or any further convincing: I was off. My computer's screensaver was about to come to life – down to a chance meeting with a stranger while buying a Buddha.

I went on to run my first Bali retreat in one of George's villas, before falling so much in love with Bali that I decided to make it my home. Years later, George has become a family friend and like an adopted uncle to me.

From the moment I met George on that chance day, I knew miracles were coming. This manifestation of my dream – of travelling to a faraway land I'd only seen in photos – reinforced to me that I could make anything I dreamed of a reality.

Travel is precious to me and for the last few years I've been fortunate enough to experience a great many beautiful places around the world. But you don't have to travel in order to find yourself. You just need to start saying yes to you, and yes to your life.

The pursuit of self-love and self-discovery is the greatest adventure you can ever embark on.

Not very realistic

It's highly likely that when you get clear on your vision, lock in some of your big dreams and start your journey towards making your dream life a reality, you'll get some funny comments, eye-rolls or people saying what they've been saying to me for most of my life: 'Hmm. Not very realistic, is it?'

When I was 15 and dreamed of being an actress, my teachers at school said, 'That's nice, Mel, but it's not very realistic.'

When I dreamed of starting a business, helping women to find freedom around food, some people said, 'Be realistic: you need a stable job!'

My new life in Bali might sound a bit 'out there' to you, but it was once just an idea in my mind – and a computer screensaver that I used to stare at. And I'm not special or different from you; this is possible for anyone, no matter what, or how big, your dreams are. You just have to believe it, and consistently show up for yourself in making them come true.

I grew up in a city with nothing really going on, my family didn't have a great deal of money and I had no connections or 'step-ups' to where I wanted to be – but I had some big-ass dreams and I was prepared to work really, really hard in order to make them come true.

When you believe in yourself and make bold moves, the Universe moves with you. When you support yourself, you will feel supported.

I say this to encourage you to live the life that you want, not the life that others say is 'realistic' for them. 'Realistic' is governed by a person's own beliefs and is absolutely no reflection of what is possible for you, in your life. Everything is realistic, if you make it so.

Don't let small minds convince you that your dreams are too big.

I spent so long feeling starved of freedom and adventure. And as much as I could blame it on other people or my circumstances, I was there the whole time, and I had chosen that life. I just hadn't been giving myself a voice, or standing up for what I really wanted deep down in my gut. I'd been burying my feelings, burying my truth, and trying to fit in. I just didn't want to upset anyone – y'know?

But trying to fit in never, ever works. It makes us miserable and depressed because we were all born to stand out. Why do you think the Universe made us each unique, with different gifts and talents, different genes, a different chemical make-up, different parents? We're not here to be like anyone else.

If you're trying to fit into what you think society wants, I'd like you to ask yourself: *Why?* Who is it exactly that you're trying to please by doing this? Is it your mum? Your dad? Your spouse? Your boss? The mums in the playground? Whose approval are you trying to win?

When you approve of your own choices, you don't need others to approve of them. You're creating your own reality. You're writing your own story. If you want to break out of your nine-to-five, if you want to break out of your unhappy relationship that you know deep down isn't right, if you want to break free from the city you live in or move away from your family, or simply speak your truth, you are only one decision away from a completely different life.

Freedom requires courage.
And courage requires trust.

We choose the walls we build for ourselves. Now, don't get me wrong, those walls have served a purpose for us for a while. They've kept us safe and in that cosy little comfort zone all this time. They've served a purpose. But maybe, just maybe, they've done their time.

You're ready.

Not next year.

Not when you've lost 10 pounds.

Not when you've saved a ton of money.

Not when all of your ducks are in a row.

How much longer must you wait?

Create your vision, lock it in, trust – and take the leap.

Don't look back, apart from to see how far you've come.

Speak your truth. You're ready – it's your time.

You've got this.

Questions to self

❖ *On a scale of 1–10, how much fun and adventure do I have in my life?*

❖ *What am I ready to start saying 'Yes!' to?*

❖ *Where in my life have I dimmed my light in order not to stand out or threaten others?*

❖ *Where in my life have I denied my big dreams, for fear of what others will think?*

❖ *I am reclaiming my dream of...*

❖ *One adventure I am committed to going on for myself is...*

We are
the ones
we've been
waiting for.

Chapter 10

Hungry for (Self) Love

*'The poverty in the West is a different kind of
poverty – it is not only a poverty of loneliness
but also of spirituality. There's a hunger for
love, as there is a hunger for God.'*

MOTHER TERESA

When we reach for food, often what we are deeply craving is love. And so often when we do this it's not about love from someone else, but rather a need for more love from yourself.

Self-love has the power to completely change not only your life, but everyone's lives – and therefore the world. If human beings knew how to love themselves, we would undoubtedly be able to live in a much more harmonious world. I can say, hand on heart, that understanding and cultivating self-love has radically changed my life for the better, and if I could give one gift to everyone all around the world, it would be this.

When we take our self-love to the next level, we begin to attract people into our lives that love us in the same way that we love ourselves. We have better friendships, we have more fulfilling relationships.

So why is self-love so freaking difficult, then? Why is it so hard for us to do? Why does it make us cringe or feel like we're 'full of ourselves'? Most of us still have a twisted perception of self-love because we have been taught that the accusation 'She loves herself so much' is a heinous crime and one we should be ashamed of. Yes, I grew up hearing that on the playground and it made me determined to never be that girl. Instead, I tried desperately to fit in, dimming my own light so I never shone so brightly that people might think I was full of myself.

If you've done a lot of adult learning in the personal development department, you probably have a good grasp on just how important self-love is. But for most people, self-love is what we struggle with the most, out of anything in life. We struggle through our relationships because we have not yet learned to be in a healthy and balanced relationship with ourselves.

It's perhaps not surprising, given that many of us grew up on movies about love stories and Disney princesses spending their whole lives longing to be rescued by a prince who would make everything bearable again – and *then, only then*, could her life really begin. This man, this one man, will fix her. He will rescue her. He will be her saviour.

Of course, as adults we can reflect back on this and clearly see that this probably wasn't the best message for us to be growing up with, and that it has profoundly impacted the nature of our relationships, without a shadow of a doubt. Thankfully, the cultural narrative for young girls is now becoming far more empowering, but we adults have had to learn the hard way that we're here to be our own heroes – and ain't nobody coming to save us.

If you're anything like me when I was a young girl, dressing up as princesses and dreaming of handsome princes on horseback, there'll be a part of your soul that died a little upon realizing that nobody is gallantly on his way to slay your demons for you, sword *et al*. No, princess, you're here to save yourself; there's nobody coming to do it for you. And if you want to meet the prince – or princess – of your dreams one day, and have a healthy, loving relationship, then I advise that you start by looking in the mirror and getting to know, accept and love… yourself. Take a look in the mirror at the person you're destined to be with for the rest of your life.

> **We can only meet each other and love each other as deeply as we have met and loved ourselves.**

As you continue on your self-love journey, you'll notice that your relationships become deeper and you're able to love much more unconditionally. You'll notice that you're able to allow yourself to be truly loved because you believe that you are truly loveable. It starts with you.

Ellie is one of those beautiful young women who can't see how incredible she really is, both inside and out. I have the pleasure and honour of working with many amazing women, but the experience is laced with some sadness when they look at themselves and cannot see what I see – or at least, not at first. Ellie was struggling with an eating disorder and didn't feel she was worthy of love, not exactly as she naturally was. She would spend hours at the gym, without food, and cancel every social event, all because she deemed herself unattractive and unworthy of any sort of a life.

Ellie was warned by her doctors that having a child could be difficult because of the damage she had done to her body from her eating disorder. On my Bali retreat, we focused on self-love and on healing Ellie's relationship with food. But of course, it's not just Ellie's eating disorder that has now been healed. 'My relationships have gone from strength to strength, and I've finally started to accept myself,' she says. 'I can love myself and receive abundant love from others."

Not only has Ellie transcended her food issues, but she has shaken off what she described as the 'prisons' of her past. She has begun to build her dream career, had some of the most difficult – but much needed – conversations with her family, and started to live life on her own terms. And she recently messaged me to announce the wonderful news that she is now pregnant. 'My body has recovered enough to give me the greatest gift in life – a baby to call my own. I know now is my time, and I'm going to grab my future with both hands.'

When we're filling the void with food, drink or some other addiction, what ought to be filling that void is self-love. It is the beginning, the middle, the end. It is everything. This is what I have learned along my own self-love journey, and what I continue to learn. We must treat our relationships with ourselves as the most important relationship of our lives. After all, we're in this relationship until death do us part. So let's make it magical.

Let's all look at what we all expect from the best relationship of our lives. What do we expect in a relationship with another that we can bring into the relationship we have with ourselves? And then, sweet goddess, let's look at how we can first love ourselves like that.

Unconditional love

If we want to be unconditionally loved by another, with all our flaws and quirks and everything else, we must first love ourselves unconditionally. This means not saying that you'll only love yourself when you've lost 10 pounds, dropped a dress size, changed your hair etc. Unconditional. Always. Now.

Trust

If we have any hope of trusting another person, we have to learn to trust ourselves. Self-trust requires forgiveness for our past wrongs and the ability to make decisions for ourselves that benefit us in the long-run, not short, impulsive decisions that cause us pain further down the line. It requires us to learn to trust our intuition, the voice we feel deep down in our gut – our inner, wisest self. Trust that you can handle all that comes your way, because you've got your own back.

Honesty

We all want honest relationships, but first we must get honest with ourselves. What are you pretending not to see? What real feelings are you denying? Where can you open up more and reveal more of the truth about who you are? When you get honest about your desires, you can own them. When you get honest with yourself about what you're struggling with, you can address it.

Loyalty and commitment

Yes, we all want partners who will be loyal to us. But are you being loyal to yourself first? Don't compare yourself to others – that's not being loyal to yourself. Be loyal to your body –

don't buy clothes that don't fit or abandon your body to idolize someone else's. Stand by your principles, remember who you are and stay loyal to yourself. Make sure you commit to doing the things you say you're going to do for yourself. You deserve it.

Communication

This is the dialogue inside your head, from yourself to yourself. Your inner-self talk. How you speak to yourself and how you treat yourself is oh-so-important. Speak to yourself with love and kindness, just as you'd speak to a friend. It starts with you. Practise giving yourself pep talks and cheering yourself on.

Time and patience

Relationships require time and patience. If you've been in an abusive relationship with yourself for a long time then you won't be able to transform it overnight; it will be a case of time, practice and dedication. You're in this with yourself for the marathon, not the sprint. A beautiful, loving relationship takes time – and you are worth every day that it takes. Be patient with yourself, just as you would be patient with someone you love.

Doing the work

Strong relationships require work and effort from both sides. And so does your relationship with yourself. Self-love is a practice and an ongoing journey, and it requires you to get honest with yourself and make the same effort that you would for a partner – and it's not all rainbows and butterflies. In relationships, you have to compromise and consistently work through things. This is what you must do in your relationship with yourself, too. It's worth it, beyond belief. You'll learn how to love and accept yourself unconditionally on all levels, and to go deeper into the relationship you have with yourself. This, in turn, will affect all of your other relationships, and allow you to welcome future relationships into your life that are deeply loving, too.

With every decision or action, ask yourself, *Is this what someone who loves themselves would do?*

An exercise to attract your soulmate

I did this exercise when I was sick and tired of attracting the wrong type of partner into my life, and I was ready for change. Just a couple of months after I did the exercise, an incredible man, named Rick, showed up in my life.

He is far from perfect – but so am I. He has his wounds from the past, just as I do. But I love this man more deeply than I ever thought I could love another, and in turn I feel his love more than I have ever felt anyone's love in my life.

This is not about finding a happily-ever-after, because that's not how life works. Disney is not real life. We don't know what the future holds, but what I do know is this: as I love myself more and more deeply, and more unconditionally, I'm able to extend the same love to this man. There is no destination: we are learning together every day, and it's not always plain sailing – but it's worth it. The more we love ourselves, the more we can love each other, and we notice that when we don't give to ourselves, we cannot give to each other. We must all fill up our own cup first, then give from the overflow.

When I revealed to my clients that I did the following exercise before I met Rick, several women reached out to me and said, 'OMG, I did this exact thing and it worked for me too!' So I'm going to share it with you here, as clearly this wasn't a one-off!

Step 1: Write a list of qualities you want in a soulmate.

Step 2: Instead of dreaming about the perfect person coming along, get to work on becoming all of these qualities for yourself – in other words, you become your own soulmate.

Step 3: That's it. That's the exercise. Go back to step 1 and repeat if necessary.

We attract what we are.

- If you are hiding from your true self, you may attract someone who is emotionally unavailable, too.

- If you are speaking down to yourself, you may attract someone who doesn't speak kindly to you either.

- When you value yourself, you will attract someone who values you, too.

We attract what we are.

So if you want to attract a soulmate who is independent, ambitious, loving, kind, wise, great at communication and able to travel, you must first become these things for yourself.

If you want to attract a soulmate who is funny, generous, heart-centred, spiritual and sexy, you must first become these things for yourself.

Questions to self

❖ *What qualities do I expect and desire from a healthy, loving relationship?*

❖ *How can I bring more of these qualities to the relationship I have with myself?*

❖ *Where have I been mistreating myself, or my body?*

❖ *A loving commitment I can make to myself now is…*

❖ *Qualities I want my soulmate to embody are…*

❖ *What would someone who loves themselves do?*

❖ *What new daily habit could I adopt, that embodies somebody who loves themselves?*

You are
the temple.

Chapter 11

What Is the World Feeding Us?

'When the Earth is sick and polluted, human health is impossible… To heal ourselves we must heal the Planet, and to heal the Planet we must heal ourselves.'

KARI-OCA DECLARATION AND THE INDIGENOUS PEOPLES' EARTH CHARTER

Let's be honest, we've been born into a world that makes it hard to be at our body's natural weight. A world that doesn't readily feed us the health, happiness and freedom that our bodies need to feel nourished and fulfilled. At least, not in some areas of supermarkets, where we find highly processed foods from companies that simply don't care if their products harm our bodies or not, as long as their products are displayed on the shelves and make money by keeping us coming back for more. These companies control the amount of salt, sugar, fat and chemicals that go into these products to make the pleasure and reward centres in our brains light up and get us hooked

Junk food becomes addictive to many of us because we have the memories from our childhood of all the salty and sweet foods that stimulated us in the past.

When we look at photos of juicy burgers or pizzas dripping with cheese, or hear the crunch of crisps in a television advertisement, our childhood memories get triggered and we want those foods.

What's more, children are targeted in the advertisements between their favourite television shows, or placed in videos alongside their favourite YouTube stars. Clever marketing tactics, bright colours and shiny, collectable toys are used to make the children believe they need to eat what the ads tell them they do, using false, empty words like 'nutritious', 'heart-healthy' and 'protein-filled' with little truth to back this up.

James Colquhoun, film-maker and co-founder of the natural food champions Food Matters, says on the company's website: 'The food industry has led us to believe that its products are going to make us healthy, happy, sexy and young. These promises are as empty as the food and drinks they're trying to sell us. The truth is we've never been fatter or in worse health.'

Meanwhile, these products are labelled and presented to us as 'food', but when we look at the labels, this so-called food consists of dozens of chemicals, preservatives and toxins that we can't even pronounce. But when these are hidden in an array of other ingredients, we don't even notice. And when it seems everybody else is eating the same thing, we go ahead and eat it, too. If justice were served, the founders of these companies that make billions out of selling us food that can making people sick should be forced to eat their own products for the rest of their lives while we all watch.

In the UK and USA, over 60 per cent of people are deemed 'overweight', 30 per cent deemed 'obese' and the food industry makes it far easier and cheaper for us to be unhealthy than healthy. Making changes to our lifestyles means we have to make a conscious effort to seek out healthy alternatives and pay extra to have better-quality, fresher food going into our bodies.

Writing in *The Guardian* in 2013, journalist Jacques Peretti says, 'When obesity as a global health issue first came on the radar, the food industry sat up and took notice. But not exactly in the way you might imagine. Some of the world's food giants opted to do something both extraordinary and stunningly obvious: they decided to make money from obesity, by buying into the diet industry.'

Lose 14 pounds in a week!

Drop two dress sizes in 10 days!

Ah, the promised land we know so well.

Peretti says, 'So what you see when you walk into a supermarket in 2013 is the entire 360 degrees of obesity in a single glance. The whole panorama of fattening you up and slimming you down, owned by conglomerates which have analysed every angle and money-making opportunity. The very food companies charged with making us fat in the first place are now also making money from the obesity epidemic.'

That's right, possibly even more fucked-up than the food industry, the diet industry takes a problem and promises to make it better, and then goes and makes it worse. The food industry makes us fat, then the diet industry sells us a web of empty promises and makes us not only get fatter, but messes with our mental health and makes us feel utterly useless at the same time.

Former finance director of Weight Watchers Richard Samber admitted to Peretti, 'It's successful because the 84 per cent [who can't keep the weight off] keep coming back. That's where your business comes from.'

Meanwhile, when we zoom out and look at the state of the planet, Earth, too, is suffering – big-time.

> **We need to take responsibility for**
> **how we treat our bodies – which**
> **are our homes – and the planet.**

The way we are treating the planet is not sustainable, and nobody wants to look at it.

If we were driving and we were to see a chicken cross the road in front of us, we would slow down and let the chicken cross. But we turn a blind eye to the slaughtering of millions of animals each day to meet the demands of the food industry. Atmospheric carbon dioxide levels are higher than at any point in human history, polluting our planet, killing nature and poisoning the atmosphere. We've chopped down more than half the Earth's forests to make more space for agriculture and factories. Sea life is becoming extinct due to our mass pollution of the oceans. Over 200 animal species become extinct every single day.

Both our body and our planet are our homes for this lifetime. Our bodies are sustained by the Earth, so if the Earth is suffering, how can our bodies, too, not suffer? Mother Earth blesses us with so many remarkable things for free: clean air, clean water, beautiful landscapes, absolutely breathtaking views, an abundance of natural foods that grow in the ground and on trees – the list goes on. We take so much from nature, but what do we give in return? How do we treat our home?

Yes, we're making huge steps forward in health and environmental awareness. Health-conscious restaurants are opening everywhere, and thanks to the Internet we are becoming much more aware of how we can treat both our bodies and the planet better. But changing the way we consume is about everyone on the planet collectively becoming more conscious of our choices and how we're treating our bodies and the beautiful planet we inhabit.

We know that we get out what we put in. If we put crap food in, we feel crap. Energy is everything, and it's no secret that your food dictates your mood. But also consider this – what else are you 'putting in'? I'm talking about what else is going into your cells. Yes, food, drink and stimulants – but also media, conversations, music, videos, relationships, Facebook, the news. What are you consuming every day, through all five senses?

We are what we consume.

The chances are, if you're feeding yourself with trash from social media, fear-inducing news articles, unhealthy, toxic relationships, drama-fuelled conversations and mind-numbing TV, this is also contributing to how you show up in the world. If you're always reading gossip, I have no doubt that you, too, are a gossip. Yes – really. I'm calling you out because it used to be me, too.

Similarly, if your kid brother spends his evenings and weekends playing video games filled with violence, guns and blowing things up, do you expect this to have zero effect on how he shows up in the world? What we consume affects us on a macro level. This is important for me to share since it has had such a dramatic effect on me and my lifestyle, too. I feel worlds away from the girl I once was, who knocked back Jägerbombs and cheap champagne on a dance floor every Saturday night in Manchester, often losing a shoe, her purse or her phone in the process, was then piled into a taxi and ferried home at 4 a.m., only to spend the next day schlepping around the flat, reading the *Daily Mail*, watching *Gossip Girl*, eating Domino's pizzas and sweets before crawling into bed.

I'll be the first to admit I used to be hooked not just on junk food, but on junk media too. Every night for at least two hours I would mindlessly numb myself watching reality TV shows while I simultaneously ploughed through an array of junk snacks. During the adverts I would scroll Twitter or look at celebrity gossip online. Is it any wonder that during this time I was also deeply unhappy, completely incapable of being in my own company and had shallow relationships and friendships? And is it any wonder that I also attracted into my life other people who fed the same demons?

Thankfully, I'm now much more conscious of my choices and of what I consume and allow into my body and my environment. I'm not perfect, of course, but I want to show up in the world at my absolute best self, so what I consume has to be aid that, otherwise it's a hindrance to it. Our health isn't just about food and exercise, it's about how we take care of ourselves emotionally, mentally and spiritually, too.

When you check your phone, what are you consuming? When you switch on the TV, what are you consuming? When you put your headphones in, what are you consuming?

It's not just about what we fill our bodies with, but what we fill our minds with.

When you log in to Instagram or Facebook, what's on your newsfeed? What's the first thing you see? Is it people moaning about their lives, wishing they were some place else, or is it people that inspire you and motivate you to be happy, grateful and make the most out of this one, precious life we have?

Nowadays, I never go out of my way to look at gossip online, and if I ever listen to the radio, as soon as the news comes on I switch over to another station. Some will say this makes me ignorant of what's going on in the world, and to a degree it is. But the way in which the news is delivered to us all is coming from fear; it's based on what is 'bad' with the world today. It encourages the listener to be shocked, to feel fear, to feel worry, to feel dread and to feel unsafe in the world. So often, what we are fed is one-sided and exaggerated by the media for dramatic effect.

Personally, I want to live in a world where I feel love, gratitude and kindness. And there's a lot of beauty in this world to take in and choose to focus on. There are also a lot of good people, a lot of kind hearts, and an awful lot of love – more than most of us are even aware of. But this rarely gets reported in the news. The beautiful acts of kindness so many humans do for each other is rarely reported or discussed publicly. Because there's not enough drama there.

> **What we consume can be our nourishment, rather than a mindless numbing agent or a distraction tool for an unfulfilled life.**

I share this just because I've been there and done that, and I know it doesn't contribute positively to the life that I, or I imagine you, want to lead. And since paying more attention to what

I consume, I also am more peaceful and happier than ever. I love and respect my body, I have no desire to be or live anyone else's life and the idea of gossip is completely unappealing to me. In turn, the people around me who I have since attracted into my life also value their growth and education, their health and wellbeing. I have deeper relationships with people because I chose to have a deeper relationship with myself. We all have a choice and we can all choose a different path if we want it enough.

People imagine it takes a lifetime to change these habits but the truth is it takes a moment. A moment in time where you see a different perspective and make a commitment that prioritizes your future instead of a need for instant gratification. We only have one life, so if your weekends are spent watching hours of TV and drinking away the pain, and your weekdays are spent at a job you don't even like, then how much of your life are you actually planning to live?

The best part is we get to decide. We get to choose what we feed ourselves every day. We get to choose what we consume, and therefore how we show up in the world.

Dieting = modern women's oppression

I want to briefly share some perspectives I've had on dieting that I think you will benefit from hearing, especially if you consider yourself an empowered and independent woman, which I hope you do.

Throughout history, we women have been made to feel we should be good and pure; we should be petite, pretty and not too outspoken; non-threatening; lovely; agreeable. *Be a good little girl. Just smile sweetly. Look pretty. Don't offend anyone. Weigh less, say less, take up less space, be less.*

In magazines, famous women are pitted against each other based on appearance and dress sense. But what about our successes, our achievements in life? Unlike those of our male counterparts, these often seem to go unnoticed.

We are taught that we females fit into one of two categories: the good girl or the bad girl; the virgin or the whore; the girl next door or the crazy bitch; the wife or the mistress; Mother Mary or Goddess Kali.

> **Promoting diet culture is a silent and subtle way of suppressing and controlling women, and making us believe we need to always be 'good'.**

Have you noticed this show up in your life, this pressure or need to be seen as 'good'? Or maybe you've identified with the rebellious 'bad girl' identity your whole life? I know how it feels to play the good girl, and it's exhausting, pushing down any sense of 'wild' – that raw, crazy, emotional goddess, that sexual, sensual, unfiltered side of me that time after time got buried away in my attempt to please others and behave as society expected me to.

And where does the 'good girl' mentality show up the most? In diet culture. It's unbelievable how many of us subconsciously start dieting as a way to fit into society, to become 'good' and 'pure'. And as a result, millions of women are distinctly ignoring their body's natural wisdom and instead obsessing to varying degrees over body size, points systems and restricting food. Because, well, everyone else does it, and we're scared to rebel against society. As women, we've been brainwashed by this culture. Why is it that when a woman has lost a lot of weight, we don't ask if she's okay? Surely, this is a concern to her health? Instead we say, 'Congratulations!' and praise her for her willpower, awarding her ridiculous titles like 'Slimmer of the week'.

Dieting is not normal. It is not our natural state – far from it. It's not the default or natural way for human beings to eat. Consuming food is something our body naturally wants to do to survive. It is a necessary function.

> **Manipulating our eating is as unnatural for us as manipulating our breathing would be.**

But entire industries make money by making us believe that we're not good enough, not thin enough, not pretty enough. The health industry, the fitness industry and the diet industry would be completely obsolete if you didn't think you were missing something they could give you. Yes, our insecurities are incredibly profitable.

Diet culture isn't just about dropping pounds. If you look closer, it's an epidemic among women that has you believe you are worthless, not good enough and totally useless without an app or tracking system to monitor yourself. Diet culture makes you believe that without rules you can't even trust yourself. Diet culture forces you to determine whether you, as a person, are 'good' or 'bad', and enforces the belief that food = morality. It completely warps your perception of 'health' and feeds the lie that thinner = happier.

At the same time that women in the West are obsessed with diet and weight loss, the World Food Programme says that close to 800 million people in the world go to bed hungry each night. And here we are, counting macros and starving ourselves because we want to fit into our skinny jeans.

It is commonly known that the majority of people who lose weight on a weight-loss diet gain it all back again – plus some on top of that. So why, why, why, I hear you cry, do we keep coming back for more? Why are the diet consultants, the ones supposedly guiding us to the promised land, also the ones who have been on and off the same damn diet for nine years, and are more miserable and weigh more because of it?

Well, because diet culture also has us blaming ourselves for 'failing'.

Take Lynnette, for example. Lynnette is a long-time member of a very popular diet club. She has been losing and gaining the same 3 stone for over five years now. When I ask her, 'Lynnette, can you not see that this diet doesn't work for you? If it did work, why are you heavier than you were to start with?', Lynnette shakes her head and says, 'No – it does work. It definitely does. I've only gained weight because I haven't been following it properly. When I stay on track, it definitely works. I just need to work on my willpower, that's all.'

Not only have we been brainwashed into thinking that diets work, we've been brainwashed into thinking that when the diets don't work, it must be our own fault.

***A one-time buyer in the diet industry is
a lifetime buyer in the diet industry.***

Because if diets did work, the industry would go out of business right away.

Dieting disempowers us, shatters our confidence, has us comparing and competing with one another and completely undermines our ability to be appreciated for our brains, our hearts and our accomplishments in life. This dieting obsession is keeping us small, self-consumed and trapped.

But we deserve to take up space in this world. We deserve to play big, not small. And we deserve a life where we get to make our own choices for our bodies, and behave like empowered women in charge of our own choices, rather than like sheep.

The masculine and feminine at play in dieting

If you're still finding yourself engulfed in diet culture and depending on it to feel in control or 'good' for even fleeting moments of time, consider the masculine and feminine energies in the Universe. Everything in the Universe has a polarity: North and South, Mother Nature and Father Culture, Sun and Moon, Masculine and Feminine. This is not about genders or to do with sex, but energies. Both masculine and feminine energies exist within each of us and show up everywhere in nature. And I imagine that at some point in your life you've recognized that the masculine and feminine energies don't quite communicate on the same wavelength. As the famous book by John Gray says, men are from Mars, women are from Venus. If I were demonstrating the energies by way of drawing on a piece of paper, masculine energy would be made up of straight lines and sharp angles, and feminine energy would be made up of curves and swirls. Both are completely different – however, one cannot exist without the other. We both have both within us, and we need the two things to be present for us to feel balanced. Just as yin cannot exist without yang, black cannot exist without white, dark cannot exist without light.

We all have an idea of what the masculine traditionally represents to us: the masculine is likely to conjure strength, protection, safety, pure consciousness, control, facts, science, numbers, problem-solving, linear-thinking, force. The masculine energy likes to fix things and achieve goals. The masculine tends to be the thinker.

The feminine energy, on the other hand, is generally seen as the 'feeler'. She represents softness, flow, emotions, patience, curvature, creativity, beauty, surrendering, spirituality, allowing, vulnerability.

> **We all have masculine and feminine energies within us, and both are forever in an eternal dance with each other.**

You may find that in your relationships you take on more of a feminine energy, but at work you take on more of a masculine, 'get shit done' approach. Or perhaps it's the other way around. There is no right or wrong way. For example, say you have a big project at work, such as designing an advertisement for a new café. It's important to understand both the design and creativity (feminine), and the structure and budget (masculine). If you focus purely on the design and creativity, you may have a beautiful advertisement for your café, but one that doesn't really communicate the message or fit the budget. But if you focus purely on the wording and outlay, you may end up with an ad that has a catchy slogan, but looks ugly. Get it?

Bringing this idea back to food, dieting and weight loss, I want you to consider that these entire industries – the diet industry, the nutritional science industry and the fitness industry – all have an extremely masculine-dominated approach. They are driven by numbers, measuring, science, facts and linear ways to 'get to a goal'. Of course, it is important to note that it is in no way wrong for women to embody masculine energy; in fact, masculine energy is what helps us to accomplish things, and can make us highly productive and driven to succeed in life. However, if you are primarily living in your feminine energy, it's likely that following these kinds of programmes has been even more of a struggle for you.

A powerful strength of the feminine energy is intuition and emotions. So is it any wonder that it's often our emotions that lead us to our decisions? We lead from the heart more often than from the head. More often than not, men tend to see food as fuel to feed the machine, whereas women tend to see it as an emotional tool – a friend, a comfort and so on.

This, along with many other reasons, could very well contribute to the reason that women tend to struggle with diets more than men do, and why women seem to have more of an emotional relationship with food than men do. In order to make a diet work successfully, a woman must take on a more masculine energy – more control and willpower, more structure, with measurements, facts and a mission to get results – which, for many of us, could feel as if it goes against our nature, which is intuitive. After all, a woman's best superpower is her intuition. This is just one facet that could play a significant part in the epidemic of diet culture and troublesome relationships with food that women face.

Questions to self

❖ *Three ways I can raise the standards of what I consume are (fill in the blanks):*

1)

2)

3)

❖ *How have I noticed myself identify with 'good girl' or 'bad girl' roles throughout my life?*

❖ *How have these identities served me and kept me safe?*

❖ *How have I noticed the masculine and feminine energies show up in my life and relationships?*

Choose
authenticity
over
approval.

'The inward journey is about finding your own fullness, something that no one else can take away.'

Deepak Chopra

It's somewhat of a paradox that, more than anything in the world, we humans long to be really seen; seen for exactly who we are, complete with all our flaws, all our imperfections – and yet, simultaneously, this is the very thing that terrifies us the most.

Are you hungry to be seen for exactly who you are? Do you even know who *you* are? When you're alone. When your partner isn't there or your friends or your mum aren't around and there's nobody to distract you – who are you then? Who are you when it's just you, alone with your thoughts?

Do you believe that person is loveable? She is.

If you've been going through your life hiding from people for fear of them seeing the real you, then you're exactly like I used to be. I didn't even realize I was doing it until I began to recognize a pattern in my life.

I don't really seem like someone who's afraid of being seen, do I? I've been an actress, and now I have a business where I'm somewhat in the public eye and always in front of a camera or on stage, shouting like a foghorn from the rooftops about self-love and making peace with food to any goddess who'll lend an ear. I don't really look like I'm hiding, do I? And if I am, I'm not doing a very good job of it!

But before the 'Look at me', 'Listen to me' and 'I've got something important to say', the truth is that for much of my life I had indeed been hiding. I'd been playing roles not just in my acting career, but throughout my real life too. I'd been fitting into the boxes that I thought other people wanted me to fit into, being different versions of myself but never all of me. If someone, usually a partner, liked a particular version of me, I would become absorbed with that version, mould myself into it and abandon all other aspects of myself. If they disliked an aspect of me, I would hide it away and reject that side of me, until I'd been doing it too long to bear it any longer.

I'd been on a people-pleasing spree, trying to please my parents, my agents, my partners. I would hide parts of myself away so I could fit into what I thought was their ideal. As I'm sure you can imagine, this was completely exhausting – but also strangely, secretly enjoyable, for part of me felt smug and like I was in control.

I've played The Good Girl, The Crazy Party Girl, The Clean-Eating Yoga Girl and The Sensible Businesswoman, all of which seemed plausible, reasonable female roles to play. At the time, each of these versions felt like me. I became engulfed in each role. But what I realize in hindsight is all of these were a type of mask that prevented me from being too vulnerable or too exposed to anyone around me. They kept everyone at a reasonable distance, stopping them from getting too close to the real me. It takes a lot to admit this, but I think it's because I wasn't fully accepting of who the real, full me was, so it felt safer to hide in one of these roles.

I realized that when I was alone by myself, I was different. Different sides of me – different sides of me that I liked – came out that I would usually hide in other people's company. I realized that I behaved differently with different people. And as if I need to tell you, this is not a preferable or a sustainable way to live.

Eventually, I was so desperate to finally play the role of myself that I broke free from all of these masks in a bid to get to know my real self. This was not a 'One day I woke up' scenario, but a gradual peeling off of masks over time, to reveal who I was inside all along. I broke up with my agent, which felt amazing; I stopped calling the friends I always changed myself to be around; and I got a divorce and decided to go and find myself. I had let someone marry the idea of me in his head, rather than the real me. Frankly, at 21 even I didn't yet know who the real Mel was, so how could I have expected him to?

At one of the Bali villas I recently lived in, I had a pet turtle named Donatello, and on becoming completely and utterly obsessed with this turtle I found that other turtles and turtle memorabilia kept showing up in my life too. Of course, as you would, I decided for myself that turtles must be my spirit animal, so I did a little research and found out a few things that rang true. Turtles hide in their hard shell for protection. Their shell is conveniently disguised to look like a rock so it can blend in to every environment on land or in the sea so the turtle can hide from any potential threats or predators. Ah, yes – that's what I'd done for years.

The journey of self-love and acceptance is a never-ending one, with many lessons and treasures to pick up along the way. It's like peeling away layers of an onion, one by one, to reveal more and more rawness, more and more *you*-ness. When I began to really accept all of those different sides of myself, including all the things I had always imagined to be unlovable, I started to feel more at peace than ever. Of course, it wasn't easy and it's definitely still something I'm continuing to work on myself.

I see you

Has someone ever looked at you and made you feel they're staring right into your soul, stripping you of all your masks and leaving you with nowhere to hide? It's fucking terrifying.

On my first date with Rick, I found it hard to look directly at him. It sounds weird, but when I looked at him he actually saw me – literally, saw me. All of me. I had nowhere to hide, no masks to assume. I felt naked and exposed (though I had all of my clothes on – promise). His bright blue eyes penetrated right into my soul and I felt truly seen. I realized later that this was because I, too, had been truly seeing and accepting myself for the first time. It was a reflection of where I had reached with how I saw and accepted myself.

Usually, on a first date, we tend to wear these masks, don't we? I guess it's normal. We protect ourselves from getting hurt. We don't want to put ourselves out there too much. We fear rejection if we expose the real us. We want to appear as cool and attractive to the other person as possible, without letting down our guard or giving any hint of the real us that we imagine to be completely unlovable and not good enough. It's an attempt to protect ourselves and to hide, like a turtle. We adapt to what we think the other person's ideal partner is and always try to stay in control. But, realistically, how long can we keep this up?

> **To risk being seen by others for our true self is to risk being vulnerable and being completely exposed emotionally.**

We protect ourselves for fear of being rejected. But by doing so, we distance ourselves from connections that are so much more real and meaningful.

This inability I had to hide from this person on day one was completely unnerving to me, but it has turned into the most raw, real relationship that I have ever experienced in my life. It's a completely different level of love, because I actually know he loves me *for me*, not just an idea of me or a role I'm playing. It's the first relationship of my entire existence that has actually seen me playing my full self, not pretending to be someone different to please the other person. And in order to be fully in this relationship, I've had to get over my fear of being seen, my fear of being completely vulnerable, completely open and completely me, which was scary. I've had to accept that I – yes, me – am loveable for exactly who I am, and that includes all my flaws and weaknesses as well as my strengths.

> *'There is nothing enlightened about shrinking.'*
> Marianne Williamson

I always remind myself of this line by Marianne Williamson if I ever find myself playing small or playing a different role in order to protect myself.

Do you love your choices, or are you choosing them for other people to love them?

Do you love who you are, or are you only that way because you think others will approve of you?

Do you even like that outfit, or are you just wearing it to please someone else?

Being vulnerable is not a weakness, it's a strength. But allowing yourself to be truly seen takes courage beyond belief. Many people go through life with a crippling fear of what other people think of them. They are terrified to have an opinion that others might disagree with, to say something that pisses someone off, to admit that we need help, to say no to something we don't want to do for someone or to stand up for ourselves. It's these people who, deep down, most want to be seen, but are terrified of judgment or rejection.

But, of course, it's always we who are our own biggest judges. Letting go of self-judgment means letting go of the need to try to meet everyone's approval, and recognizing that in order to live a truly full-up life you aren't going to be able to make everyone happy. In fact, you're highly likely to rub a few people up the wrong way – and that's okay. Find the tribe that gets you, and get naked (metaphorically speaking, not physically, although I do recommend that, too).

Being vulnerable means being prepared to get emotionally naked. Getting naked is brave but it's strong. And when you've done it once, you realize that, actually, it's pretty damn liberating. What's more, when we let down our guard and allow ourselves to be truly seen, it can lead to some of the most beautiful, treasurable moments of our lives.

***In order to be seen for who we truly
are, we must first see ourselves – see
ourselves with unconditional love
and acceptance of who we are.***

Who we *really* are. Look into our own eyes and really see the person looking back. See through the eyes of your soul. And accept and be with that person. That person is the one you're sleeping with every night of your life. That person is the one you're in a relationship with until you die. What aspects of her have you been rejecting, that you can reclaim?

Don't be afraid of your own light, your own power or how magnificent your life could really be if you show the world the real you.

The world has been waiting for you – it's your time.

Using the body as a shield

If you have excess weight on your body that has felt impossible to shift, it's there for a reason. Just like everything in the Universe, it serves a purpose. And although you may only have cursed it and blamed it before wishing it would go away, there could be a reason it's there that you have perhaps not been able to see yet.

There is a positive reason your body thinks you need the weight that you do have. For many people, extra weight is not because of a lack of nutritional intelligence, greed or anything to do with genetics.

***Excess weight can often be the external
result of a much deeper internal issue.***

Many of us wear excess weight as a shield, for protection. Bodybuilders will relate to this, too. Gaining excess weight – fat or muscle – creates a 'bigness', a 'power' and a type of armour for the individual to wear so that they feel safer from danger and from others taking advantage of them. Often people go into bodybuilding to build a bigger body so they can feel more powerful and to be able to protect themselves, and this can be due to a trauma in their childhoods, perhaps one they experienced when they were so young that they don't even remember it. It's the same for excess weight and obesity – it's often the result of a deep, internal need for protection. Although gaining weight doesn't heal the trauma that already exists, it acts to suppress anger, resentment and pain, and acts as a layer of safety and protection against future traumas. So your weight may be there for a positive reason for you. It may have served to feel like your safety, your protection.

Diets or training plans won't work for very long for these people because the reason the excess weight is there in the first place isn't being addressed or resolved. If the individual has encountered sexual trauma, weight gain can also serve as a subconscious way to minimize sexuality and attractiveness to an outsider, in the belief that today's society finds thin people more desirable. This is used as protection against further sexual trauma or abuse, and to a degree it makes the person feel like they are 'hiding' and not being seen, which helps them feel safe. The person doesn't want to draw attention to themselves and believes that the bigger they get, the more invisible they get. But this isn't the case, and ironically the body is instead becoming more visible to you, saying, 'Look at me!' and demanding that you give it the attention and the care that it craves from you.

Mary Anne Cohen, director of the New York Center for Eating Disorders, writes, 'Many survivors of sexual abuse often work to become very fat or very thin in an attempt to render themselves unattractive. In this way, they (subconsciously) try to de-sexualize themselves. It is their attempt to feel more powerful, invulnerable, and in control so as not to re-experience the powerlessness they felt as children.'

The key to resolving this is to access and heal the wound with love.

> **Be gentle with yourself and remember
> you're not to blame, and you're
> most certainly not broken.**

We live in a world where most people are trying to address the symptom of their problem (by going on a diet, drinking the shakes, starting a training plan, having more willpower) rather than the actual root of the issue, which is why for many people the weight doesn't stay off. It will stay off only when you're able to come to terms with the fact that you're now safe in this world, you don't need your body to protect you any longer and you can allow yourself to walk towards your fear of being seen again.

When you make choices for your body to feel better, from a place of love rather than a place of hate, and not by trying to make your body different from what it is, and begin to deal with your emotions face on, rather than using food as a way to bury them, this is when your body will naturally let go of excess weight.

Letting go of the weight

In order to release weight, we must identify what is emotionally weighing us down, and become lighter by releasing it. When people are happier all-round in their lives, and feel like their life is in alignment, they tend also to free themselves from the extra baggage they've been holding onto, baggage that may have shown up as extra weight. Extra weight can often be stored as emotional energy in the body. Of course, I want to add that weight loss is most certainly not the key to happiness, just as more money or more followers on social media aren't. But for the purpose of this chapter, let's talk about successful weight loss.

There are two types of weight loss that commonly exist. The first type is where the individual tries to attack the symptom, not the problem. This involves the hard slog, willpower and seemingly impossible task, where everything feels like an uphill battle and the weight you lose never seems to stay off for more than a short while before it's back on. This kind of weight loss is perpetuated by diet culture and consumes our lives by having us tracking and measuring calories or macros, making the person feel like they're in a constant fight and most of the time completely miserable. This person is always asking themselves, 'What can I do to lose weight? What are all the things I should be doing? Eating less? Working out more? Drinking less? Cutting out sugar?' This person wants control, rules and systems. This type of weight loss is what most of the population are trying, but more often than not they end up heavier and unhappier than they were to begin with.

The second type of weight loss is the effortless, natural type of weight loss. This is when the individual is actually addressing the root problem causing their excess weight, not the symptom. The individual is consciously or subconsciously changing their relationship with food, healing the relationship they have with their body and choosing to make loving choices for their body because they wants their body to feel better. This person develops an awareness of their emotions, and recognizes the patterns and habits behind their using food for reasons other than when they are hungry. This means the person is able to understand their relationship with food and to stop the patterns themselves by acting from a place of love and nurture for themselves and their body. This person doesn't rely heavily on measuring or tracking anything, because weight loss becomes a natural response to the body reducing its frequency of over-eating or emotional eating. This person is pursuing a fulfilled, healthy life, rather than simply pursuing weight loss. This person starts to lovingly address the areas of their life in which they do not feel fulfilled, and their relationship with food mimics how they feel about themselves. The more they fall in love with themselves and their life, the less they use food as a crutch or substitute for love.

The first person, who is obsessively trying to lose weight, goes about it by hating themselves until they're thin. The second person is not completely consumed with weight loss at all, but may naturally lose weight as a byproduct of becoming aware of their relationship with food, understanding what it is they are really hungry for and becoming healthy by loving themselves. The first person focuses on what they have to do in order to lose weight, but the second person focuses on the person they want to become in order to live their very best life. One person is purely focused on changing their body, while the other person is focused on changing their life.

In order to lose weight, we must first find peace with our weight. Only when we truly accept our weight can we begin to release it. Our relationship with our own body is crucial here, because if you're fighting what exists, you're resistant to it and it will be much harder to lose. If your relationship with your body is one of hatred, punishment and shame, then you are in resistance to what is.

Before you can release your weight, you must accept what is, see it fully and be with it. Dr Marc David, founder of the Institute of the Psychology of Eating, puts it like this: 'In order to drive a car, you have to first of all get into the car. You can't drive the car without getting into it first.'

In other words, get into your body before you want to drive it anywhere. Be in your body; be with it. It's yours. Fall in love with everything that exists now and recognize that it exists for a reason. Only from this place of acceptance of what is can you move forward.

You don't have to lose weight to be seen in all your glory – you have to be willing to see yourself.

Lizzy works as a journalist and her work often leads her to be invited to glamorous events and photo opportunities. But I know as well as she does that when you're hiding yourself from the world and battling your body, all photos – no matter how glamorous they appear – have negative connotations. 'They were all tied up in memories of diets,' she says, recalling herself looking at the images. '"This was when I had lost a stone…"; "This was when I came off *Slimming World* and was bingeing like crazy…". My food and weight tarnished everything, as if all of those photos are tinted grey.'

Lizzy joined my Academy to heal her relationship with food – and now? She describes her life as 'technicolour' – and best of all she didn't have to change herself to reveal her true self to the world and to bask in all her marvellous glory. Through healing her relationship with food, she was able to fall in love with herself and her life again. She was hungry to be seen by the world, and the world was hungry to see her, too.

'Now my memories are happy days, new experiences, joyful achievements and, yes, food – but wonderful, celebratory, shared food. Happy food, with no baggage. I'm getting married in April and I'm so excited that these pictures will show a girl who is having the best damn day of her life, whatever her shape or size.'

Questions to self

- *Where in my life and relationships have I been hiding from my true self?*

- *How has this protected me? What good has come from this?*

- *How has it stopped me from living my fullest life?*

- *Where in my life is people-pleasing showing up?*

- *Where in my life have I chosen approval over authenticity?*

- *What parts of myself have I been rejecting? Why?*

- *One thing I can do this month to reclaim that side of me, is…*

The Masterpiece

When a man looks upon a piece of art, he marvels in its glory.
The structure, the brush strokes, how it speaks to him.
How it touches his soul.

Its uniqueness is truly remarkable.
Its heart is so real he can almost feel its pulse.
This, this is pure beauty.

The man does not walk in close, inspect the art and exclaim:
'There appears to be one brush stroke that is
not in-line here! This displeases me!'
The man does not walk in close, inspect the art and exclaim:
'This art does not align with all of my own
beliefs and opinions! This displeases me!'

The man simply marvels at the masterpiece.
And lets the masterpiece be.

It may not be 'traditionally' beautiful to everyone.
It may be somewhat confusing.
It may be sometimes controversial.

But it is real.
It is raw.
The masterpiece… is you.

The only
way out
is in.

Chapter 13

Hungry for Deeper Meaning

'It is absolutely a relationship with food that is a displaced relationship with God. And that displaced relationship with God takes two forms: our availability to other people and our availability to our own thoughts and feelings.'

MARIANNE WILLIAMSON

When I was younger, I was fascinated by other worlds. As a child, my first obsession came with mermaids, and for hours a day I would assume the role of the Disney character Ariel. I was utterly convinced that a world under the sea existed and that I, too, was a part of that world. Every visit to a beach would see me going home with a suitcase full of shells (and sand) that I had collected on my wanders along the seashore.

Next came a fascination with crystals. At the age of 11, I would save up my pocket money to buy the magazine *Mind, Body, Spirit* from my corner shop. I didn't pay much attention to the articles as I couldn't fully grasp most of them, but the magazine would give away crystals and tarot cards on the front, which I would collect, and this was my treasure. My bedroom in Coventry had a huge bay window, and I taped a large bedsheet to the ceiling and draped it so the bay window section of the bedroom was partitioned from the rest of the room. This would be my meditation den. I filled this area with cushions and with the treasures I had collected – incense, tarot cards, crystals and all kinds of other weird and wonderful things that I had no real idea how to use, but treated as my prize possessions. I would play meditation CDs in my Walkman and try to meditate in my den, sitting on my cushions. I imagined that if I did this for long enough, one day I would begin to levitate. Much to my disappointment, this didn't happen. I tried really hard, though. I didn't share this with any of my friends at school. It was completely uncool.

One time I had a very vivid experience with a spirit, in my childhood home, a very old Victorian house. I woke up in bed to see a figure of a soldier at the door, looking straight at me – it then ran out of the window and disappeared. I had never been so terrified in all my life. My mum later described ghosts she saw regularly in her room after her mum passed away. After that I wasn't scared; I was curious. My mum was extremely open-minded and also supported my crystal and tarot habit without asking many questions.

Next came a fascination with astrology. Every school lunch break, without fail, I would be on the computer looking at my daily horoscope. That horoscope would significantly determine my actions, especially if I fancied a boy in my class (and if our horoscopes weren't compatible it was game over).

I loved being this girl. She believed in magic and played in a little world of her own. Unfortunately it wasn't long before this part of me got put to one side.

As I grew up and started becoming more interested in boys and make-up,

I began to realize that this spiritual hobby of mine wasn't cool or attractive.

I began to get more pocket money and spent it on clothes and hair straighteners. I stopped buying *Mind, Body, Spirit* and instead bought *Star* magazine and *Heat*, where celebrities were pulled apart for having cellulite on the backs of their legs or compared against each other on the beach, with articles asking 'Who weighs what?' I saw images of beautiful Hollywood movie stars on red carpets and then I saw them ranked 1–10 based on how well they'd chosen their outfits, 10 being 'Wow, we all approve of this!' and 1 being 'How could she ever have considered even leaving the house?'

I saw stars going through anorexia being glamorized on the covers, and stars who were more curvy being shamed. You may remember the 'Size zero' phase that swept the celebrity world and impacted millions of young, impressionable girls (long before the Kim Kardashian era of big lips and big booties). Nicole Kidman, Mary-Kate Olsen, Paris Hilton, Victoria Beckham – all displayed the 'lollipop head' look and cemented my belief, and that of many other young girls, that the thinner you were, the more you were successful, worthy and approved by society. This was a dangerous world to be a teenager in. The more magazines I would read, the more I began to validate myself based on my appearance.

Some days I would spend hours straightening and styling my hair, and putting on make-up, for school. My skirt got hitched up higher and higher. I began to skip my lunches and lie to my mum about what I ate. The meditation den was ripped down to make more room for hair products and make-up. And it wasn't long before the memory of that curious, spiritual moon-child was put in the closet.

**Do you remember who you were before
the world told you who you should be?
Do you remember that curious child
who got lost in her own world?**

We've all experienced the synchronicities of the Universe, though many of us deny it. We've all had experiences that we can't quite explain, or that have felt like we're being 'looked out for' by someone or something. We've felt it. We can't explain it, but we just know it's there.

What if we weren't human beings who believe we sometimes have spiritual experiences? What if, instead, we were spiritual beings *having* a human experience? And everything is not what we experience through our five senses. What if there's more? There's so much about this world that we can't explain, or that's not how it first appears to be. We all say that the sea is blue, but none of us can go to the sea and collect a bucket of blue water. The sea is not blue, it just appears to be blue. We all say that the sun 'rises', but the sun doesn't rise – the Earth rotates in a way that makes the sun appear to rise. So what if our collective view of ourselves is not what it appears to be? What if we're not 'he', 'she', 'you' or 'I' – what if we're all pure consciousness, expressing itself in remarkable ways on this planet for a short time – as human life?

Are you breathing right now, or is breathing just… happening? When a thought appears in our awareness, is it we who think that thought?

When you close your eyes and hear a voice giving you a running stream of thoughts inside your head, who is that? Is this voice really you? No: the thought just appears. If you are the one thinking, then tell me, what is your next thought going to be? Similarly, we do not choose our thoughts, though we can choose whether or not to believe them. We are just the witness of our thoughts; we are just an observer. If this stuff is confusing or overwhelming for you, I get that. Trust me, I do. You don't have to understand fully how the magic works, you just have to smile and acknowledge the fact that there is magic present.

While recovering from my eating disorder, a huge part of my work on this was learning to surrender and ask for guidance. Ask for guidance from who? I didn't know. Just from a higher power. I would often pray, and ask for signs that I was on the right path, following my intuition and challenging my former beliefs.

Instead of constantly trying to change my physical body, I realized that I am so much more than just my body. I have a body. My soul lives in this body. I love this body. But I am not this body. When my body dies, I do not die. So why am I spending my life trying to have 'the perfect body'? What use is 'the perfect body' to the world?

Only through digging into healing my relationship with food and having awareness of myself was I able to access this realization and fully feel it to be true. Only through healing, surrendering and releasing control was I able to reconnect with my spiritual self, the self that I had been denying all along. Through healing my relationship with food and my body, I was able to reveal my relationship with the Universe, or God. And now I'm able to feel truly guided and held by that. I'm able to feel safe, and that the Universe really does have my back. And the only way to attain this trust is simply to… trust.

Kristina is a personal trainer from Sydney who attended one of the retreats I hold in Bali. As a teenager, she had been really curious about what was then called 'New Age' spirituality. She was so drawn to it that she got a part-time job in a store that sold Tibetan clothing, incense, crystals and a treasure trove of other mystical amulets. 'It made me feel free and supported to experiment, explore and curiously discover "me" within the world.'

Throughout her twenties, Kristina found herself in friendship circles that, over time, dimmed her light. She lost confidence and began to fall into spirals of self-loathing. A few years later she had developed an eating disorder. By then, her spirituality was long forgotten and dismissed as a fad – 'just the fantasy-land of a stupid little girl'. What followed this was three years of obsessive calorie counting, over-exercising and restricting and denying herself food. She finally began to seek help, and her therapist recommended *The Goddess Revolution*. This is how we met.

Through healing her relationship with food, Kristina has not only rediscovered a positive relationship with herself and her body, and remembered how it feels to truly love herself, but she has also rediscovered that teenage girl and her love for the spiritual realm. 'I was able to return to parts of myself that had become lost and buried by the obsession over my weight, and the intense control I sought over my life.'

Spirituality cannot be practised when one isn't willing to surrender control and give in to trusting something greater than us. In learning to intuitively trust her body, Kristina was able to trust me in helping her, too, and to return to the truth of who she had been all along. She began to feel whole and complete, without turning to controlling food as a mechanism to achieve this. She began to create a spiritual practice that suited her. 'I meditate, and journal my gratitudes whenever I remember or whenever I feel I need a positive reground. I even see my car sing-alongs as a spiritual practice! The point is, spirituality is available to all of us once we do the work to stop controlling what we "do" and start exploring the way we "be" instead. This work started from a desperate and dark place to overcome my food and body demons, but it ended up giving me so, so much more.'

How is this not magic?

You think this is a coincidence, that you're here on this planet that happens to be exactly the perfect distance from the sun to create just the right atmospheric conditions to keep us breathing? You think it's some kind of a coincidence that you have those parents, that you had that childhood, that upbringing?

The chances of you just being alive are so… incredibly… slim. You realize that, right?

The odds of becoming a human being are 400 trillion to one. 400 trillion to one! Yes, that's right! You're more likely to win the lottery 10 times in your life than you are to become a human being. WTF? With these statistics, why aren't we all absolutely grabbing our lives by the balls? Why aren't we all going after our big, scary dreams? We have this one, precious life. Do you realize how special that is?

There are 8 billion of us, each unique and different from each other – every single person, every single soul, every single body – with no two of us the same at all? You think that's by chance? It's nothing short of incredible, that's what it is. How is this not magic?

The Universe functions in absolutely perfect alignment with itself. We are all living on a gigantic blue rock made primarily of water and spinning on a giant axis in space, kept alive only by a massive burning star floating miraculously in a galaxy in the infinite Universe.

You have trillions of tiny cells in your body, all perfectly made and working every single day to keep you living, breathing, loving. How is that not magic?

You think this is an accident, the path you find yourself on? You think God dealt you a bad hand? You're a miracle, goddess. No mistake.

You think your quirks and uniqueness are imperfections? You think they're flaws? You think it's an inconvenience that your bodyweight fluctuates from time to time? That you gain a few extra pounds here and there? You think it's an accident that you were born into this body? This life?

Oh, hell no. Out of all the people in the world, one man and one woman came together, and out of all the sperm – millions of tiny sperm – one of them made it to the egg to create the magical, wondrous being that is you. *You!* Wow. How is this not magic?

You think that's some accident…? You think the Universe made some kind of a cock-up? No, babe. There are no accidents here.

You think God made a mistake with you? Put you in the wrong body? Put you here to suffer in your stories?

You think it's an accident that you experienced that shitty relationship? After all, wasn't it that shitty relationship that led you to appreciate a good one? How is that not absolute magic?

Is it not extremely profound how our cycles sync up with other goddesses we spend time with?

You think it's an accident that we experience changes in ourselves when the moon changes?

I mean, how are we not magic?

I mean, sometimes don't you just think, *What the...? How is this not magic?*

Out of all the millions of women in the world, and out of all the millions of books in the world, you found *this* one.

You think that's some accident? You think that's some coincidence? Ha!

Magic.

What if it's perfect?

Every struggle you've ever experienced, every breakdown, every heartache, every time you questioned how you would ever make it through the day, every time you got rejected and swore to all of your friends you would never go back to that person for more pain – but then you did and it hurt even more than the first time; every time you ugly cried into a large glass of wine that may or may not have turned into a bottle, every time you ever lost someone you love, every time you questioned your purpose on this planet ... What if it's all perfect?

What if everything in your life that ever caused you to cry into your pillow was actually perfect?

What if all of these things weren't happening *to* you – what if they were all happening *for* you? What if all of them have been perfectly leading up to this very moment, this very version of you? And all you have to do is simply see the beauty and find the hidden gems within the mess. Find the diamonds in the rough. Find the lessons within the bad times. Watch how that experience led you to grow.

If you ever experienced a dysfunctional relationship with food, like I did, or an unhealthy relationship with alcohol, drugs or anything else… What, you don't think that's perfect, too? You think that's some kind of a mistake, an accident, on your path?

Sure, you can go through your life believing that. But what if it's actually all perfect?

When I was living with bulimia, it completely consumed my life. My abusive, addictive relationship with food controlled me and made all of my decisions. I hated myself, I had no self-worth and I believed I could never feel any different. I believed that that was it: I would live with these demons forever. A couple of half-arsed attempts to visit a counsellor didn't 'fix' me (surprise, surprise), so it looked like I was stuck living in my little self-created hell. Every day I would go through the same addictive patterns: restrict, binge, purge; restrict, binge, purge; restrict, binge, purge… Some days I would lock myself in my room all day just so I didn't have to face food. Some days I would take sleeping tablets, just so I would fall asleep and not be able to eat.

Some days I would binge until I actually passed out from the pain. I would spend most nights in agony from the abuse I was inflicting on my body through these patterns, as well as through my laxative addiction, which caused never-ending griping pains in my stomach, that I then masked with painkillers. I lost any sense of the vibrant, confident Melissa I'd been before. I pushed my family away, isolated myself from friends and became best friends with my addiction instead. In those days, I barely knew who I was anymore. Fast-forward to now: I have learned how to fully love and embrace myself and my body.

I have made peace with food, and now truly make the most of my life on this planet. I have grown a business reaching thousands of women and helping them to love themselves deeper and heal their relationship with food, too, and to go on beautiful journeys of personal growth. Doing this work, I have never felt happier, more free, more purpose-driven.

So what?

Well, if I hadn't followed my pursuit of acting, if I hadn't been to those depths of darkness with my addiction to food and diets, if I hadn't been on that exact journey, then I wouldn't be the Mel I am today. I wouldn't be half as happy or as free as I am now. I wouldn't be as confident, as loving, as carefree. I wouldn't be as sure of myself. I wouldn't feel as good naked.

But I had to do the work to get here. Had I not gone to those dark places, I would never have arrived here in this dream life I have created for myself.

What if it was all perfect – all along?

When we see it's all actually perfect, not only can we make peace with the past, but we can actually be extremely grateful for it. Without it, who would we be?

After my divorce, I realized that I was developing some patterns around men that didn't serve me. I seemed to be unable to call in anyone loving or healthy for me. Instead I chose guys who had a history of cheating, made me feel anxious, were emotionally unavailable or were known as being a bit of a dick.

I realized that I was the only one calling this into my life, and continuing to tolerate the same sort of people with the same behaviour. I had to take responsibility and write a new story. I put in work to love myself deeper than I thought possible so I could stop attracting unloving patterns. I put in work to make myself feel safe in the arms of my own love so I would stop running away from commitment. I decided to commit to myself. I immersed myself in my own spiritual and emotional growth. I took my self-love practice to new levels. I faced my fear of being alone. Really alone. And I became my own soulmate.

Months later, I met an incredible man who provided me with an opportunity to break my destructive patterns for good. We created a beautiful relationship together, based on friendship and a real, deep, intimate connection. Passion and sex were the icing on the cake – not the cake itself.

My point?

Had I not experienced the bad relationships, I would never have become my own soulmate. Had I not experienced that anxiety, heartache and pain, I would never have brought awareness to, and healed, my own relationship wounds and issues. Had I not been prepared to look at that and take responsibility for what I was attracting, I would never have eventually attracted a great match.

Not only can I now make peace with this part of my life, but I can actually be *extremely thankful* for it. So thanks to all the guys who treated me badly, who caused me pain, who weren't a fit: you helped me so much on my journey. You made me truly know and appreciate real love.

What if it really was perfect?

Trust – and believe – that everything is always for your greater growth, and for your highest good.

It *is* actually all perfect. It's all so freaking perfect, you have no idea.

So relax.

Honour Mother Nature

Look around you at this absolutely breathtaking planet we live on.

Look.

No – *really* look. See it. See the oceans. See the waves, which effortlessly crash up and down the beach 24 hours a day, governed by the moon, without humans needing to control them. See the beautiful beaches, made from trillions-upon-trillions of microscopic grains of sand. See the stars in the sky, mesmerizing and fascinating us beyond belief. See the magnificent clifftops, the hills, the lakes, the trees. See every flower; really look into every single flower – designed to absolute perfection, with exquisite symmetry. Not controlled by humans, but birthed effortlessly by Mother Nature.

See the fish swimming in the sea, see a blade of grass, see a fruit, a growing plant or a herd of antelope galloping across the plains. Breathtakingly, soul-captivatingly beautiful. Be absolutely in awe of nature. Then recognize that you are part of it. Yes, *you* are just as captivatingly beautiful. We are nature. Absolutely everything on this planet is connected to each other – including us. We are part of the Earth, just as the trees, the animals, the skies are.

It's little wonder that we feel most connected when we get into nature. When we go to the top of a cliff, we can't help but stare out and feel connected to ourselves. When we go to the ocean, we stare out into oblivion, reflecting on life, asking for answers and receiving them – because we feel connected. When we go for a jog in the park, or we sit on the beach, or we lie in the grass – we feel connected. We feel peace. Because we're at one with nature, and by getting into nature we remember *our* true nature.

When we're disconnected from nature, we're disconnected from our own nature.

If you feel disconnected right now – in your body, in your life – get into nature. Do you have any nature in your environment? Or are you spending all day, all week, indoors and glued to technology? Ask yourself how you can invite more nature into your life. Instead of going to the gym, try going for a run in the park. Instead of partying this weekend, head to the beach. Go climb a mountain. See how much more connected you feel – to yourself, to others, to the world – when you make the effort to get into nature.

It's not surprising, then, that we feel best in our bodies when we are *consuming* nature and natural foods, when we eat in tune with Mother Nature. Dieting and mass-produced and packaged foods are the result of humans trying to control nature. But when we consume energy that has grown in the ground, or on trees, we are fuelling our cells with nature. It is who we are.

Foods that are readily offered to us by Mother Nature are our healing partners. These are the foods that our bodies truly thrive on. Go to Mother Nature, rather than Man, for your answers. See how much more connected you can feel. We can learn to work with nature in so many ways. The sun feeds us energy and light; it keeps us alive. Try waking up when the sun rises, and try going to rest when the sun sets.

The moon governs our emotions. Notice whether you feel more emotional during a full moon and more reserved when there's a new moon. Use these energies to work with the moon. Notice the beauty and accuracy of astrology, and find out where the planets were aligned at your birth. You are part of this vast, beautiful Universe, and you are connected to the sun, the moon and the stars.

> **Our bodies are designed to work with nature. When we gain unwanted weight, it can often simply be linked to habits that are going against nature.**

Research has proven that our bodies metabolize our meals most effectively when the sun is highest in the sky – around noon. Yes, our bodies are attuned to the precise rhythms of the sun! So try eating your biggest meal around this time, rather than late at night when it's dark. Similarly, when the sun has set, allow your body to rest. When the sun sleeps, you sleep. And when the sun is up and about, so are you. See how it feels to adjust your rhythm to be in tune with the sun.

Like eating in the middle of the night, or eating big meals very late in the evening or eating unnatural foods, dieting, too, goes completely against our nature. Controlling and restricting foods, manipulating our weight and our body, then overeating at the weekend. Why, we should ask, do other animals on this planet not try to change their bodies to be like something they're not, or go on restrictive diets only to binge at the weekend? These animals know who they are; they honour their true nature, and the way they eat is a part of the way they live and breathe – intuitively, moment to moment.

Look at the beauty that is the seasons. Every year we experience spring, summer, autumn and winter. This is no accident. This is necessary for our environment to operate. Recognize the seasons within yourself, too. Since you are part of nature, you will also experience seasons. You may be someone who has been in 'summer' season for a long time – constantly on the go without any rest and recuperation. Or perhaps you've been in hibernation for many seasons, feeling like you're always in your 'winter'. Whatever season your body is in right now, honour it. Recognize that it's just a season, and seasons have to pass.

Questions to self

❖   *Where have I rejected my spiritual self?*

❖   *What have I been drawn to learning more about?*

❖   *Why have I resisted this? Who am I afraid will not approve?*

❖   *What in the past has caused me pain that I can now be deeply grateful for? Why?*

❖   *One way I can get more in tune with Mother Nature is…*

Chapter 14

Hungry for Pleasure

*'If someone does not want me it is not the
end of the world. But if I do not want me
the world is nothing but endings.'*

NAYYIRAH WAHEED

Our relationship with pleasure is confused – and confusing.

What comes to your mind when I say the word 'pleasure'? Even the word is pleasurable: *pleeaassuure*. Yet many of us have been brought up to believe that many pleasures are 'bad' or 'sinful'. The term 'guilty pleasure' is carelessly thrown around, making us feel like we don't deserve pleasure until we've worked really hard to 'earn' it – and we then experience an aftermath of shame or resentment. Some people even believe that pleasure is pure evil or that it's deemed as lazy, indulgent, something to be punished for.

Worse still, for many of us pleasures such as sugar, alcohol, sex or drugs have associations with downwards spirals. The pleasure they give may be only momentary, fleeting, perhaps an escape from pain; or it may be a constant distraction from the numbing feeling that something is missing.

But hold on a second – if pleasure is so goddamn awful, then why does it feel so good? When we eat a piece of chocolate cake, why do we have to preface it with, 'I'm soooo bad for doing this'? Why can't we just eat the damn cake and enjoy it without condemning ourselves? We're eating cake, for heaven's sake, not robbing a bank.

And why did the Universe give us the ability to experience pleasure if we were supposed to condemn ourselves for it every time? Pleasurable food, pleasurable music, pleasurable touch, pleasurable sex. Of course, as with everything, it's not *pleasure* that gets us into trouble, but our *relationship* with pleasure that can lead us astray.

> **The ability to feel pleasure is what
> we were born with; our bodies
> understand and desire pleasure.**

Contrary to what society would have you believe, pleasure isn't something we have to earn or feel ashamed about. Pleasure can be nourishing, delicious and guilt-free, without needing to be earned – and we can find true, lasting pleasure simply from our lives and from ourselves.

Pleasure is a part of our make-up. It's our birthright. And food isn't designed just to sustain us, but to also give us pleasure. If you've been having protein shakes for breakfast, garden salads for lunch and a tin of soup for dinner, have you perhaps forgotten what it feels like to have a pleasurable food experience?

A lack of pleasure, of course, adds to the ever-growing tower of reasons why diets don't work – because they reject and cast aside the basic human need for pleasure. Diets reject pleasure from food as a basic human need and have you fight against your cravings, demonizing them instead. Look at how much the term 'guilty pleasure' shows up around food. Don't even get me started on how a popular diet club uses the term 'syns' to measure how 'badly' you've behaved around food and how much you'll have to redeem yourself later on the treadmill, you bad, bad girl, you.

But you deserve to receive pleasure. You deserve to have things in your life that nourish your soul and bring pleasure into your life. Yes, you deserve to spend time on things that give you pleasure.

Food and sex

There are a tremendous number of links between food and sex, and of relationships we can have with each of them. The human need for food and sex are a huge part of our nature: we need to eat and we need to procreate. There are no higher desires for the human race. Both eating and having sex are part of our intrinsic make-up, and most of us think about food and sex multiple times in a day. Both are extremely intimate acts, and when we eat and when we have sex we're not just tasting: we're using all five senses. Food and sex appeal to our deepest pleasure points – arousing, sustaining and nourishing the most important parts of ourselves, and both acts release dopamine, the feel-good, pleasure hormone.

Having an active sex life is good for the body. Having great sex gives you a great complexion (you know, that after-sex glow) and a good amount of sex is a cornerstone of a healthy lifestyle. Having orgasms helps your body grow tissue, balances your hormones and boosts fertility.

So, the good news is, if you love eating food and having sex, then you're completely normal. But what if your relationship with food and sex isn't so rosy? What if you're at war with both food and sex? Due to their connections, it should come as no surprise that many of us who have challenges with food, also have challenges in the bedroom. If you haven't been allowing yourself to feel pleasure from food, you may not have been allowing yourself to receive pleasure in the bedroom either – perhaps you're always pretending you've got a headache or you're too tired. This, often paired with a lack of love for your own body, means it's no surprise that you don't want to get it on.

Maybe you're someone who denies herself any form of pleasure in food, or feels guilty if she has it. Meanwhile, when it comes to your sex life, perhaps you're still holding onto bitter resentments, find it hard to trust, or think sex is overrated in relationships anyway.

Maybe you're getting all the right 'nutrition' but no sense of real nourishment or pleasure from your food. When we eat really fast, we tend to skip all the pleasure. Slowing down is key. And this is the same for sex. When we do it really fast, we skip loads of pleasure. Taking your time is key if you want maximum pleasure from your love-making – or from your food.

Making love to food

Enjoyment is key. Creating an experience out of mealtimes is key.

Let's imagine a young woman exploring Rome, and she stops to have lunch at a restaurant on the side of the street. She orders spaghetti then reads her book and watches the city go by. When her spaghetti arrives, she enjoys every single mouthful, tasting it all, licking her lips and delighting in its flavours. This, to her, is a pleasurable eating experience. Another example could be me going to my favourite dessert place in the town of Ubud in Bali, taking in the ambience and ordering the most decadent raw cacao truffles you can imagine and devouring them slowly, tasting every last bite and feeling truly nourished and satisfied afterwards. Both are incredibly pleasurable eating experiences, in my opinion.

The opposite of these two scenarios would be wolfing down spaghetti from your lap while you're scrolling your phone or scoffing chocolates while you're on your commute. Same food, but entirely different eating experience. Pleasure versus very little pleasure.

So which experience do you consider healthy for you? Which do you think will help your body metabolize the meal and make you feel nourished? When you're mindlessly scoffing, not present and receiving no pleasure; or when you slow down, taste everything and allow the food to truly pleasure you?

Eating food can feel like making love – or it can feel like a quickie.

Food is more than just nutrition: it's a defining human experience. But so many of us have been taught that it's a sinful, shameful thing to receive pleasure from food. We often do it quickly, in private, standing up, in a hurry, eat-the-chocolate-cake-while-your-face-is-still-in-the-fridge-style instead of setting the scene, sitting down and enjoying it slowly. Pleasure.

Sharing food, using food to celebrate and to bring the tribe together, dates back thousands of years. Cooking for someone is a way to show your love for someone, or to impress them. Take a look at the 'candlelit dinner' and what that represents, for example: good food, good company, good ambience, hopefully leading to… good sex.

Food and sex are intrinsically linked through pleasurable emotion. What's also fascinating to note is that it's during our teenage years that we begin to discover the pleasure of sex, yet it's often during these years that we also begin to see sex as 'bad' and 'sinful', and believe our sexuality to be shameful or embarrassing. I remember losing my virginity and feeling ever so ashamed and embarrassed about it. I thought it meant that I was dirty, that I had instantly lost my purity. Maybe you remember some of the same feelings from your teenage years.

These teenage years also mark the start of most eating disorders, a problematic relationship with food or at the very least an awareness of diets and which foods are 'good' or 'bad'. And it's during these years that we become conscious of which pleasures give us feelings of guilt and shame.

Welcoming real pleasure back into my sex life came around the same time I welcomed carbohydrates back into my life. Allowing myself to receive pleasure from delicious food again was revolutionary for me. It was bloody wonderful.

If your sex life is looking a bit glum right now, I invite you to take a look at how much pleasure you're allowing yourself to receive when it comes to your food. Am I saying that having more pleasure around food could lead you to having more pleasure in the bedroom? Why, yes I am.

Pleasure is not evil – it's our <u>relationship</u> with our pleasures that can become a problem.

They don't have power until we give them power. When we prioritize our addiction to our pleasures over everything else important in our lives, or start to heavily rely on them for relief from pain, that's what creates a problem. One burger won't make you sick, but your desire to eat a burger every day could well do so. One night of kinky sex won't make you sick, but if your desire to seek out and have kinky sex every day is disrupting your relationships – well, that sounds like a problem to me.

Stop and ask yourself these questions:

Do you allow yourself to receive and experience pleasure – whether from food or from sex?

If you have a love–hate relationship with food, do you also have the same love–hate relationship with sex or other pleasures?

Junk sex, junk food

Junk sex is the same as junk food. It's known for tasting good at the time, but it leaves you feeling dreadful afterwards. It's instant gratification for an impulsive desire that in the moment sweeps you away and gets you temporarily high, but leaves you feeling empty and deeply unsatisfied. Like sleeping with someone who you know isn't good for you: you get to the end and you're like, *Ugh, I wish I hadn't done that.* Or like eating a Big Mac – going through a McDonald's drive-thru, in and out as fast as possible, get it in, get it done, throw away the wrapper and remove all traces of evidence that this event ever occurred. *Pretend it didn't happen. Wipe it from your memory.*

Engaging in one night of junk sex won't derail you – just as eating one Big Mac won't. But both of these can be highly addictive when this becomes a habit. Both leave you feeling disgusting. No matter how much junk food you eat, you get no real satisfaction or nourishment from it. And no matter how much junk sex you have, you'll never be satisfied or feel good from it. It's soulless sex. You feel that you've given someone a part of yourself that you'll never get back.

> *Just like junk food, junk sex starts with an attraction, a craving, a lust. You get literally high off the experience of it. You want more, more, more, continually chasing that high – but then you feel sick afterwards. Disgusted with yourself and consumed with regret.*

Today's culture has, to a degree, glamorized junk sex just as we've glamorized junk food. Many young people sleep around casually, not really considering the implications or the detriment it has to their ability to be truly intimate in a relationship when the time comes. And, simultaneously, many of us are mindlessly eating junk food throughout our daily lives, not really considering the effect it has on our long-term health.

Soulful, sacred sex

During my first year of separation, I experimented with my fair share of dating and allowed myself to come alive sexually again, to figure out exactly what turned me on. I dated different types of men, but never got too close to anyone because I wasn't ready to *really* let someone in. Anyone I dated was kept at a decent arm's length. Deep down I longed for real connection and intimacy, but the thought of being completely seen by someone absolutely terrified me.

Getting over my fear of letting my guard down, and allowing myself to be truly seen for who I was, was a key part of my learning to release control and to allow real intimacy back into my life. It took my self-love to new levels, because I realized that self-love is not all about pampering yourself. Sometimes, self-love is about being really honest with yourself (in a loving way) and shining a light on where you are in pain, and it's often brutally hard work. Doing this kind of work isn't always a walk in the park, I've learned.

Over time, I relearned how it felt to be intimate with myself; to fully be with all aspects of myself and all my emotions. To love myself unconditionally, even the parts that I thought were undesirable. To touch myself; I began to remember how it felt to enjoy my body's capacity for pleasure. Real, lasting pleasure – not just junk-food pleasure. I learned how to satisfy my emotional needs as well as my sexual desires, and my healthy appetite for deep, meaningful, full-bodied sex returned. I welcomed pleasure in all forms into my life without guilt or shame afterwards.

Now, the more open I become, the more I learn and the more I reveal about myself. The more I open my heart, and my capacity to love myself, the more I have the capacity to love others deeply, beyond anywhere I'd ever dreamed of. Not only has this opened me up to new levels of love and intimacy, and soulful, sacred sex with a man I love, but it has also opened me up to a deeper spiritual connection. But to get here, first I had to get completely naked emotionally. Completely open. Completely vulnerable.

For women very much occupying their masculine energy (control, willpower), it can be hard to accept real intimacy and pleasure because it means surrendering control. It means becoming vulnerable, letting your guard down, being completely seen. And, for many of us, handing over control is scary. Control is the thing that gets us places, helps us achieve so much. But it can also turn into suffering, hard work, struggling, pushing, pulling, stressing. Achievement without fulfilment is the ultimate failure in life – and so is a life without pleasure.

I have realized that, truly, the more intimate, deep and loving the connection you have yourself and with the Universe, the more you can be intimate and have a deep, loving connection with another person. And the stronger it is away from the bedroom, the stronger and more intimate it will be inside the bedroom. Emotional openness leads to openness in the bedroom, and that real intimacy and connection is truly what creates the most soulful, sacred and mind-blowing sex you could imagine.

> *'The orgasmic experience connects you with your spirit, reorganizing and revitalizing your cells... The hormones released during sex alter your brain wave patterns toward balance and integration, activating the awakened cosmic mind.'*
>
> Barbara Marciniak

For this type of cosmic, soulful sex, both beings must be deeply intimate and connected to their true selves, and be fully prepared to be completely open and intimate with each other. Full, deep orgasms require emotional intimacy, surrender and trust. It makes perfect sense that orgasms are a vehicle for you to connect with God. Have you ever experienced anything so otherworldly as an orgasm? You are literally transcending your human body for a moment in time and allowing your consciousness to enter another realm.

Caitlin is a goddess I'm close to who has been on her own journey with spirituality, and with her sexuality, too. During the Bali retreat, she revealed to me that she had a great relationship with her husband, but things in the bedroom weren't as good as they could be. There were higher levels of intimacy they could go to with themselves and with each other.

She recalls, 'My sex drive was zero. I felt so unsexy and undeserving of pleasure. I thought I didn't deserve an amazing sex life and that I definitely wasn't sexy. But it turned out it was just another thing for me to control.'

Caitlin began re-inviting pleasure into her life, with food, with herself and with her body. First she had to realize that she was also worthy of an incredible sex life, and mind-blowing orgasms. 'Once I realized that I actually deserved an amazing sex life, once I let go of that control and just surrendered to pleasure, all those limiting beliefs just disappeared. And now? Well, let's just say there are no complaints in the bedroom!'

It starts with you

Get intimate with yourself. Know your deepest, darkest fears and your biggest secrets. Be honest, and don't play games with anyone, including yourself. Be real. Raw. You. Stop rejecting yourself, decide to love and accept the shit out of all parts of you. Rediscover your love for your body, and decide right now that *you are enough*. Not only are you enough, but you are deserving of your own sexuality and your body is your temple of worship.

Your time to love your body is now – so treat it in a way that makes you feel sexy. Adorn yourself. Pamper yourself. Wear the fancy underwear. Bypass the treadmill one night to go to a dance class instead. Just do what it takes to make you feel like a goddess. Get intimate with your body and turn yourself on with touch. Your body is your playground. Your deepest most relaxed state is necessary. When a woman is turned on, she is in her power. Attune to your spiritual self, regularly meditate and journal, and be in deep inquiry with yourself and with God.

Own all of your desires, in all areas in your life.

If you're a teacher, but deep down you dream of becoming a health coach, own your desire. If you're a vegan, but sometimes you just really crave a fillet steak, own your desire. If you really love men, but sometimes you love women, too, own your desire.

Practise surrender. Do not try to control your food, your relationships or your partners. Control is not sexy. Losing control, however, is.

It doesn't matter if you haven't met 'The One'. Sex with someone who isn't 'The One' can be amazing too. Allow yourself to be fully intimate and open with yourself and with your partner, so you can connect on a deeper level. Listen to your own sexual desires and express them to your partner. Tell him or her what feels good and what doesn't. Let them tell you what feels good for them. Communicate with each other. Don't go silent.

Sexual energy is creative energy. It makes us want to make stuff (like babies, or art). Sexuality is the highest form of transmutable energy. We have the ability to transfer our energy here into other areas of our life for the purpose of achieving our desires and dreams.

Allowing true pleasure and intimacy back into your life should feel like you are reconnecting with the divine, sacred feminine: the Goddess, in all of her glorious form.

The Goddess does not search outside herself for answers, for she knows all of her answers lie within.

She is confident and wise.

She is in touch with nature, and with *her* true nature.

She knows how to receive full-bodied, lasting pleasure.

She knows she is worthy.

She is in touch with all aspects of herself.

The Goddess doesn't promise herself that she'll love herself only when she has lost 10 pounds.

She loves herself now.

She knows her power.

She knows she is the entire Universe.

Sex is not a dirty sin. It's a powerful experience, bringing two souls together in vibrational harmony with one another and with the Universe.

Pleasure heals us. Pleasure is our birthright.

Questions to self

◈   *What is my relationship with pleasure?*

◈   *What feelings do I associate with pleasure?*

◈   *Do I notice any correlations between my relationship with food and my relationship with sex? What is interesting about them?*

◈   *How can I invite more pleasure into my life?*

◈   *What desires have I disowned that I am now reclaiming?*

◈   *What turns me on most about myself and my life is…*

Turn yourself on.

Chapter 15

Hungry for Creativity

*'Follow your own fascinations, obsessions,
and compulsions. Trust them. Create whatever
causes a revolution in your heart.'*

ELIZABETH GILBERT

The lovely man I'm now with, Rick, grew up an extremely creative child, obsessed with art and drawing. At school he loved creative writing and storytelling, and showed disdain for any lesson that wasn't art or drama. But later, as a teenage boy, he felt the pressure of society to 'make it in a man's world'. He chose to cast aside his love of the arts (creative, feminine, right brain), and instead chose a more sensible-looking career in business that seemed to promise a higher and more stable income. He created a successful career in the fitness business, heading up a huge protein company and achieving ample recognition. But (you know where this is going) he felt that sinking feeling, that something was missing. In a stressful, high-powered work environment, everything had become about control (masculine), and anything creative or emotional (feminine) felt too messy and unpredictable, and like there wasn't enough time for it. Have you ever had this same feeling?

'At the same time that I was denying the creative aspect to myself, I was also denying the feelings within myself,' Rick says. 'I was feeling less, but thinking more. I had more success, but less happiness. It was like I was a prisoner of my own life. I felt numb.'

Three years following this realization, Rick now creates his art for a living: he travels the world filming and directing extraordinary visual pieces, and combines his love of visual art with his passion for storytelling. But to get there he had to have the courage to admit that the path he was on, in business, was simply not fulfilling him anymore.

For me, creativity is about performance. Whenever my mum invited guests over, little Melissa would without fail bust out her Capezio tap shoes and put on a solo dance routine, kicking her feet up past her head, twirling in her jazz pants, grinning like she was on Broadway and giving her best show-stopping moves, while the guests sipped their tea, pretending to be wowed by yet another one of Melissa's performances to the Spice Girls.

In my early twenties, I rejected the acting industry because I was so consumed with my food addictions. My eating disorder was cleverly masquerading as a passion for nutrition, so I followed that instead, abandoning the performer in me. In time, and now that I have a business I created from scratch, I have been able to choose ways in which I can bring back this performer, in small ways, to the here and now – via on-stage speaking events, and creating videos for YouTube. But still, that side of me has largely remained buried. Until now.

I recently gave a TEDx talk in Switzerland, on self-love and healing our relationship with food and our bodies. Prior to delivering my talk, I worked on it with a coach. The first time I gave my talk in front of her, she said, 'Okay, Mel. Here's the problem I see: you're a performer, and as soon as you get on that stage you go into performance mode! Your comfort zone is your drama training. But that's not what we need. We need *you*.' I completely got it. I diligently took her notes on board and focused on just speaking from the heart, as if the audience were just one person. This seemed much more authentic, and I was pleased with the changes.

Having arrived in Switzerland for the event, Rick and I had dinner the night before the big day. There had been rehearsals earlier, and I asked him honestly if he thought I was still 'performing' a bit too much. It seemed like as soon as I got on stage, I just couldn't help myself – I loved it, I thrived on the energy. He answered, 'Mel, yes – maybe a bit. But look, it's who you are. You are a performer. Don't deny that aspect of yourself. It's part of your soul.' I reflected on this. I recalled my childhood days of dancing, singing and acting, and how it would make me feel, and as that sense of elation came back into my memory, tears started streaming down my face. I had been rejecting that side of me for years, focusing solely on my business.

As I write this, I am making a commitment to pursue this side of me again, get back into drama and dance classes and reignite my creative spark for performance and acting. I cannot deny that it's a big part of who I am deep down, and terrifying though it is to me – since that industry is where all my demons first reared their heads – I am willing to face those fears head-on with the work I have now done on myself, and the tools I now have, and reclaim that creative inner child that I have rejected for so long. Is there a creative child in you who you've been forgetting too?

Dancing with the fear

I'm not implying that you pack in your job and pursue a career in the arts. But what about your inner child? What did she love to do when money wasn't even in the arena? Before society told you who you should be, before your teachers told you which university to get into and your parents told you which subjects to study? What did you love to do just to express yourself, with no attachment to the outcome? Could you make room in your life now for that inner expressive child that got cast aside during the journey towards your sensible, adult life?

Remember, just like flowers, we are here to fully express ourselves before we die, and for someone to suppress themselves and their creativity is a crying shame for humanity. Suppression can often lead to depression, and as we know, suppression of feelings can also show up through your body, sometimes in the form of addictions or distractions, when we are not getting our deeper needs met.

We are at a critical time in history and the Internet has completely changed the game for creative expression for all of us. Now, for the first time ever, we have all been given a free platform – a voice, a creative outlet, a way to share our gifts with the world. In seconds we can say or post something that has the power to impact thousands of people's day.

Technology can support your creativity. There's never been a better time than now to get creative and share your gifts with the world.

Whatever your message, whatever your passion, you now have the ability to create an audience for it, share it and show it off.

So what holds us back from expressing ourselves? Oh, yes – fear. Fear of what other people will think of us: what our parents will think, what Julie from across the road will say; what your old friends will think; what your work colleagues will make of you.

Fear keeps us safe, but also a little too safe. It keeps us cosy inside our comfort zone – also known as 'the place where zero growth happens'. So, thank you, Fear, for keeping me safe up until now. But you are now dismissed.

Something fabulous happens when someone allows themselves the time and space to creatively expresses themselves. It radiates out of them like beams of light, and everyone wants to be around them. We just love seeing people do what they love. It lights them up, and it lights us up too. So instead of worrying about what everyone will think of you, realize that when you pursue your own creative passions, you'll also be inspiring others to pursue theirs. A knock-on effect of you doing what you love is that you're actually helping other people do what they love in the process.

Do it even if you're crap at the beginning. Do it even if it's embarrassing. Do it even if you fail or people laugh. Do it even if what you do doesn't change anyone's life. Do it even if it doesn't make you money. Do it even if nobody notices.

Just do it… to do it.

**Scale down your workload and make
time to express yourself creatively.**

Go to an adult ballet class. Take up pottery on Tuesdays. Learn to style interiors or fashion. Try photography. Go to an oil painting workshop. Start singing again. You don't need to change the world with it. You don't need to win awards for your creativity. You don't need to reinvent the wheel. Just express yourself. Have a love affair with your creative passion – at the weekend, on a rainy day, in the evening. Spend less time down the pub or on social media (unless you're posting about your passion – heck, what is Instagram if it's not a platform for creativity?), and spend more time getting those creative juices flowing! Just do it because it just feels good.

Of course, you don't miraculously have empty hours to do that, and nobody wakes up one day and knows how to write a book or play the piano. You need to take your time – so make time.

After the initial excitement of writing *The Goddess Revolution* and preparing for it to go to print, I instantly fell into a pit of 'not good enough'. I called my editor, Amy, from a Starbucks one day and had a wobbly – my inner bitch was coming out loud:

Who are you to share this message?

You're too young. Nobody will value your advice.

What a load of shit this is!

Through my tears, I said, 'Amy, I don't know if I'm good enough for this. I'm worried it's rubbish. Should I change it? What if people hate it?' Amy comforted me and said calmly, 'Mel, you are definitely good enough. It's definitely not rubbish. And this is your message. You must share it with the world.'

Our egos love being the star of the show and thinking they're at the centre of the universe, but if you've got a message, or a piece of art, it's not really about you, *per se*. You're the vessel, the vehicle, the artist, but once your art is out in the world it's not your baby anymore.

I just needed to express the message that profoundly changed my life and that I hoped would get into the hands of other women who really needed it. It wasn't up to me if other people liked it or not, just like it's not up to you if other people like your particular creative expression or not. If people leave negative comments about your beautiful jewellery creations, or tell you that your raw, gluten-free food tastes gross, simply smile and remember: it's not your job to please everyone. Just express yourself. It doesn't matter if someone has done it before you, or if you're just starting out, or if there's competition. Just stay in your lane, and *do you*.

To close this chapter, I'll leave you with another story from my Bali retreat. Every evening before bed we have a 'Goddess circle' ritual. One of the ladies I had the privilege of hosting on this particular week was Lillie. Lillie has such a vibrant, infectious personality, with a love for pandas and the ability to make anyone smile at any time of day. You just wanna squeeze her.

When she arrived on the retreat, Lillie revealed to us that she had recently overcome an eating disorder. Unable to focus on anything apart from her body, she had become involved in physique and body-building competitions that saw her starve and dehydrate herself under the guidance of her coach. She was only 20 years old.

'I didn't like the person I was, or the body I lived in,' she recalls. 'I didn't feel worthy of anything. I didn't feel I deserved to be happy and live in abundance. This outlook on life also held me back from my dreams of writing a book and pursuing my passions. I can now say all of those things are in my vision, and if they're not in my vision it's because they're happening in reality.'

Midway through the week, during one of the goddess circles, Lillie pulled out her bag, and out of the bag came 12 individual pieces of calligraphy. She had asked for each woman's favourite quote and carefully scribed these onto paper, with gorgeous watercolours to finish. Everyone was in tears. 'Lillie, this is incredible!' we all exclaimed. 'You're so talented!'

Ever since her food issues began, Lillie had pushed her natural creative talents under the carpet, being consumed instead with counting macros and controlling her weight. She came to Bali to finally say goodbye to that life and start anew with a fresh perspective on food and her body image. When Lillie had realized that attaining the perfect body wasn't her purpose in life, she realized she could get really curious and explore the sides of her that had been pushed aside. Finding calligraphy was not just a welcome distraction during her eating disorder, to focus on something other than food, but it played a key part in her coming home to herself.

Now Lillie creates her beautiful calligraphy pieces for gifts, is travelling solo as she always dreamed of doing and has even begun to write her book. 'The biggest affirmation I made to myself was to be the creator of my own success. I am creating the life I want, I have unleashed my inner child, I have taken a leap of faith, fallen crazy in love with myself and now I truly know that miracles are possible for me.'

This is your permission to create, dear goddess.

Questions to self

❖   *When I was a child, I expressed myself creatively through…*

❖   *I stopped this, because…*

❖   *My favourite way now to express myself creatively is…*

❖   *When I don't make room for creativity, I feel…*

❖   *What fears hold me back from living a more creative life?*

❖   *What new ritual could I introduce to my life that will fulfil my creativity?*

How your life feels is more important than how it looks.

Chapter 16

Hungry for Connection

'We're hardwired for connection. It's what gives purpose and meaning to our lives. The absence of love, belonging and connection, always leads to suffering.'

BRENÉ BROWN

Connecting with others is intrinsic to our nature. All we have to do is look at where technology is today to see how important it is for us to be able to connect with others. Technologically, we are more 'connected' than we have ever been in history: we can send a message to someone on the other side of the planet in less than a second. We can join meetings over video calls, broadcast to thousands of people from our own homes and hear people talking to us on mobile phones from several continents away as clearly as if they were standing next to us.

And yet, we feel more disconnected than ever. Many of us lack real connection in our relationships, real connection with ourselves. We are so hungry for connection that we spend all day glued to our phones – but in turn we don't know how to have real conversations anymore. We find it awkward opening up to people. We freak out when we don't have Wi-Fi, but when our friends call us we think, *OMG, don't phone me!*

The ability to feel connected is how we're wired and why we're here. We're longing to feel more connected but in our search for connection we're becoming disconnected from our true selves. Many of us can't stand to be anywhere, or even in our own company, if we do not have a phone in our hand. Anxiety and depression in teenagers is the most common it's ever been. The rate of eating disorders is also at an all-time high.

Suicide rates are also at a record high: according to the World Health Organization, more than 800,000 people die from suicide each year – that's one every 40 seconds, and more people than die annually in war and natural disasters combined. But instead of spending trillions of dollars helping those affected to get support, treating the root causes of this depression and suicide and helping them find a better connection, we're ploughing that money into war and arms, which only creates more separation and disconnection.

We cannot turn our heads the other way and act like this is not a problem. The problem is that we are searching for connection in all the wrong places. Connection is what gives us a sense of belonging. And when we feel like we don't belong or we aren't good enough, this is when we feel disconnection.

As I'm writing this, I am recalling a very special dinner last night, which I will never forget. Rick and I took my mum and stepdad Shaun out for a meal for their last night here in Bali. As the four of us sat round the table with our food, the usual small talk occurred: talking about Bali, talking about the food, talking about work, talking about what we'd been up to recently and talking about how lucky we'd been with the weather, since it's rainy season right now, which makes the weather here very unpredictable. The conversation turned to Rick, and he began to share some insights into what he'd been working on recently. He shared a little, then stopped. I urged him to share more. I urged him to share his big dreams with my parents.

I could tell this made him feel uncomfortable because opening up more would make him vulnerable. But he took a deep breath, and he shared with my parents his biggest dreams, of becoming an artist – the dreams that have always scared him, how he felt about it and why it was so meaningful to him that he did this now, after all this time of not doing it and pursuing other businesses instead. He opened up to my parents about where he'd been, his past, his childhood, his fears and how he conquered them and continues to do so.

The vulnerability he showed to my parents allowed them to connect with him on a deeper level than they had before. He let them in – I mean, really let them in – and before I knew it, both my mum and Shaun began to open up more themselves, revealing their deepest vulnerabilities, too. I learned more that night about my stepdad than I think I've known in the last 17 years. I connected with him on a deeper level than I had ever done before. Why? Because he allowed himself to be truly vulnerable. And vulnerability creates real connection. It requires courage, so much courage, but if you're longing for real connection in your relationships, you have to dare to go there. It sets you free, and in allowing yourself to be vulnerable, you give others permission to do the same, and this forms real connection in your relationships.

Brené Brown, an author and research professor studying vulnerability and courage, defines connection as 'the energy that exists between people when they feel seen, heard, and valued; when they can give and receive without judgment; and when they derive sustenance and strength from the relationship'. But in order to experience real connection, we have to be prepared to be truly seen, as our true selves. This is where we need to get radically real, deeply authentic and honest with ourselves.

Remember Johann Hari's response to his research on addiction: he said the opposite of addiction is not sobriety – it's connection. What those rats were missing when they got hooked on the drugs was connection. If you feel disconnected from the people you love, or like you're craving a deeper connection, it's up to you to go there. Get vulnerable. Get real. Allow yourself to be seen.

Connection with yourself, with others and with a higher power is where it's at. I, personally, feel most connected to myself, and to my body, when I'm practising yoga and meditation. I feel connection to others when I allow myself to ask for help, to be vulnerable and to be truly present with that person. When I quit the small talk, and ask, 'How can we go deeper here?' – that's where the real goodness lies. And when I get by the ocean, or up onto a cliff top, in the mountains, or watching the moon and stars at night, I feel connected to Mother Earth, and connected to a power greater than myself. What about you?

Questions to self

* *When in my life do I feel most connected?*

* *What is it in my life that leads to me feeling disconnected?*

* *Where do I find myself turning to, when I feel disconnected?*

* *One thing that I can do more of to deepen my connection with self is…*

* *One thing that I can do to deepen my connection to those around me is…*

* *Follow what makes your soul come alive.*

Chapter 17

The World
Is Hungry
for You

'Stop acting as if life is a rehearsal. Live this day as if it were your last. The past is over and gone. The future is not guaranteed.'

DR WAYNE DYER

Finally, here are 30 of my favourite ways to lead a truly fulfilled life that I have found completely invaluable throughout my own journey of discovery. They have helped my soul to enjoy soul nourishment, and helped me to regain my appetite – for life.

Be present

Instead of replaying the past or worrying about the future, be fully in the here and now, which is all that truly exists. Trust that you are exactly where you need to be. Be present with yourself and give others the gift of your full presence.

Be self-aware

Become aware of your own thoughts, feelings and reactions in particular situations. Notice when something excites you. Notice when something agitates you. Notice what emotions you experience and when. And when something does come up, be it a negative belief or habit, rather than judge it, ponder it with a curious, inquisitive approach. Question everything. Become fascinated with getting to know yourself on a much deeper level. This is key.

Love and respect yourself

Accept that you are a miracle and there is only one of you in the world. Choose to love yourself, honour yourself and respect yourself. How you show up for yourself is how others will show up for you. Realize that exactly where you are now is exactly where you need to be.

Pursue your passions

Allow yourself to be guided towards the things that make you curious, that make you tingle inside – the things that light up your soul. This is where you will lose yourself – and find yourself.

Follow your big dreams

Believe that your imagination creates reality, and that no dream is too big to realize. Lock in your vision. Be specific. Set the bar as high as you want and the Universe will build you a ladder.

Get out of your comfort zone

Cosy as it may feel, your comfort zone is where zero growth or change happens. If you want to experience big shifts, you have to be prepared to step outside that comfort zone. We don't grow from being comfortable but, rather, from getting comfortable with being uncomfortable. Everything you've dreamed of is waiting for you – but it's all outside your comfort zone.

Make bold moves

Also known as 'Massive aligned action in the direction of your dreams'. Be a little bolder. Sometimes, jump in at the deep end instead of dipping in a toe then shimmying in through the shallow end. Sometimes, dive bomb. Make a bold move.

Make time for loved ones

Relationships are at the heart of our lives and what we all value the most. Prioritize your family and friends. Make them know how much you appreciate and love them. They won't be here forever.

Bask in gratitude daily

Every day, bask in a state of gratitude. Look around at what you have, this incredible life we get to live and this remarkable planet. Be in awe of it. Give thanks for the food on your plate, for hot water, for a bed to sleep in every night. Be grateful for your ever-evolving journey and how it's leading you to places you never imagined you'd go. Be grateful for your support network. Your dance classes. Your dog.

Don't take life too seriously

Know when to chill out and be able to laugh at yourself. Allow yourself time to play, have fun, dork out and take the piss – especially out of yourself! Take a break and go surfing, or blast Beyoncé and dance for no reason. Tickle someone until they cry. Laugh until your belly hurts. Live more.

Only compare yourself with previous versions of you

Comparison is a one-way ticket to a black hole of self-despair. Instead of comparing yourself to other women, see them as your sisters and allow them to inspire you to become the greatest version of yourself. If you ever must compare, compare only to older versions of you, to see how far you've come.

Make loving choices for yourself

Ask yourself regularly, *What would someone who loves themselves do?* Make choices for yourself that come from a place of love. Eat, sleep, talk, think, drink, dance, all from a place of love.

Look up from your phone

Self-explanatory. The good stuff happens when you look up. Don't miss it.

Find a deeper connection

Connect with yourself regularly through meditation, journaling and self-reflection. Be prepared to go deep with yourself. Talk to God. Talk to yourself.

Rediscover your creativity

Paint. Draw. Sew. Bake. Write. Dance. Design. Whatever it is that gets your creative juices flowing, carve out time to do it.

Listen to your gut

That knowing in your gut is usually right. Don't ignore it, or it will only grow louder. Pay attention, and honour it.

Say yes to adventure

Always. Especially if it involves you trying something new, or challenging yourself to grow.

Be of service and contribute

Focus on what you can *give* to others, not what you can *get* from others. This is key for a truly fulfilled and happy life. To be of service is to become bigger than we see ourselves. Our attention shifts. We set aside our preoccupation with ourselves and turn our focus outwards, towards others and a higher purpose than our own needs.

Look after our planet

Reduce your carbon footprint and use less plastic. Recycle and pick up litter. Support sustainable energy movements and vote for leaders who prioritize climate change. Treat this planet as our beautiful, incredible home. She is our mother. She is who we are. Do not take her for granted.

Let go of trying to please everyone

It's impossible to live a life of authenticity without pissing off a few people along the way. Drop people-pleasing. Stay true. Be you. Speak your truth. The right ones will stick around.

Stay on your mission

Be so focused on your mission that you don't care what others are doing on theirs. Stay in your own lane, and stay on your own game.

Challenge your beliefs

Question the stories you tell yourself. Ask yourself where your beliefs come from. You get to decide what you choose to believe. You are writing the story of your life.

Forgive yourself and others

Forgiveness sets us free. If you want true freedom, forgive yourself and forgive others who have wronged you – set them free, too. And remember that we all fuck up from time to time, don't we?

Believe in yourself

You are capable of absolutely anything you put your mind to when you believe in yourself. Those who believe they can change the world are usually the ones who do it.

Visualize daily

Create your vision, lock it in and visit it every day. The more you imagine it, the stronger that relationship with The Future You becomes. Daydream often. Know that all of your dreams are on their way to you. Own your desires and make bold steps towards them.

Look for the lessons

Within all of the failures, look for the lessons. Each perceived failure contains at least one hidden lesson – this is the gem and it's your job to find it and grow from it. With this approach, you won't give up, and will be constantly learning along your journey.

Be solution-orientated

Instead of focusing on the problem at hand, focus on finding the solution. Solution-oriented folk find the answers, but problem-orientated folk usually find more problems.

Judge less, love more

We cannot love and judge someone at the same time – and that includes ourselves. When we love ourselves more, we judge ourselves less. When we judge ourselves less we are able to love other people more and judge them less, too. Everyone wins.

Let go of perfect

Know that perfect is an illusion and a never-ending game that never leads to true happiness. When you drop the need to be perfect, you allow yourself to be you again.

Celebrate the journey

Don't wait for milestones or goals to celebrate yourself. Celebrate every step of the journey and every lesson you learn along the way. This is where the real beauty and magic is. Don't forget to stop and do a happy dance. You deserve it.

Live a full-up life

Falling in love with you is possible.

Changing your life is possible.

Becoming free is possible.

Coming home to you is possible.

Believe it.

Trust it.

Write your story.

Own your desires.

Embody your vision.

And have courage, dear goddess.

You've got this.

Acknowledgements

Thank you to the whole team at Hay House UK, USA and Australia for all your help with writing, editing, printing and marketing this book, and for all the support you have provided to me as an author and speaker.

Thank you Emma, Sarah, Alana and Laura for all your help behind the scenes, not just with this book, but with every other moving component of the business. You are each so invaluable to me. Thank you to Hannah Verdun at Verdun PR for helping this book get out there into the world.

Thank you to Jackie, Shaun and Charlie for your support, and to Hannah, Persia and Bry.

Thank you to Dr Marc David, Marianne Williamson, Elizabeth Gilbert, Dr Brené Brown, Dr Wayne Dyer, Russell Brand, Deepak Chopra, Kris Carr, Patricia Lynn Reilly, and every other teacher who has provided endless inspiration to me over the years along my journey.

Thank you to Rick, for your unwavering support, for all of the play during work hours and for seeing and loving me exactly as I am.

Most of all, thank you to my goddesses far and wide: to my Academy goddesses, my retreat goddesses, the goddesses who follow me online and the goddesses who have been with me since the very beginning.

Thank you to every single reader who has been called to pick up this book. I deeply appreciate you.

ABOUT THE AUTHOR

Bry Penney

Mel Wells is the bestselling author of *The Goddess Revolution* – described by *OK!* magazine as 'the body bible' – a TEDx speaker and Health and Eating Psychology Coach. She's helped thousands of women to heal their relationships with food and their bodies, and then go on to create truly fulfilling lives, falling in love with themselves more than they thought possible.

Mel has been featured in *Women's Health*, *Cosmopolitan* and *Glamour* magazines, and on Forbes 30 Under 30 and BBC Radio 1. She works with women one to one, and through her online Academy and retreats around the world.

f iammelwells

𝕏 @iammelwells

◎ @iammelwells

www.melwells.com

HAY HOUSE
Look within

Join the conversation about latest products,
events, exclusive offers and more.

 Hay House UK

 @HayHouseUK

 @hayhouseuk

 healyourlife.com

We'd love to hear from you!